Your Freudian Psychoanalysis

. . . in five hours, not five years

Your Freudian Psychoanalysis

. . . in five hours, not five years

Anthony Dugdale

PSYCHE BOOKS

Winchester, UK
Washington, USA

First published by Psyche Books, 2012
Psyche Books is an imprint of John Hunt Publishing Ltd., Laurel House, Station Approach,
Alresford, Hants, SO24 9JH, UK
office1@jhpbooks.net
www.johnhuntpublishing.com
www.psyche-books.com

For distributor details and how to order please visit the 'Ordering' section on our website.

Text copyright © Anthony Dugdale 2012

ISBN: 978 1 78099 763 6

The intention of this book is to provide accurate general information about the subject
matter covered. It is not the intention of this book to render professional services to the
reader. If the reader requires advice or expert assistance, the services of a competent professional should be sought.

Design: Stuart Davies

Printed and bound by CPI Group (UK) Ltd, Croydon, CR0 4YY

We operate a distinctive and ethical publishing philosophy in all
areas of our business, from our global network of authors to
production and worldwide distribution.

Contents

Acknowledgments

Numerous books written about Freud made it easier than it would otherwise have been to summarize his work; some of the most influential are listed in the Bibliography and further reading section.

A very special thank you to Judy Spours, who patiently provided me with invaluable editorial advice and feedback. Likewise Marcia Williams who, as well as encouraging and cajoling in the nicest possible way, has been a true friend. Thanks, too, to all those students who taught me so much about Freud over the years.

BEFORE you lie down on the couch . . .

When Sigmund Freud opened the door marked "UNCON-SCIOUS" in the mind, reached his hand into the darkness and switched on the light, the pattern of human thinking was changed forever. This book will show you how you can relate some of Freud's most important insights into the human mind to yourself—and how you can recognize some of the more improbable parts of his theorizing. It will explain why some people become gynecologists and other people become executioners, and why Freudians consider ballet dancers and the people who watch them to be perverts—except in name. It talks about why people campaign to save the whale, dye their hair, enjoy hurting themselves, shift blame onto other people, choose unexpected partners, become vegetarians, wear flashy ties, convert to religion, suck their thumb, choose bread-making as a hobby, or believe in magic—Freudian theory is nothing if not ambitious. There are twenty-eight Freudian questionnaires here, each one designed to enable you to develop a Freudian insight into yourself by revealing what unconsciously motivates you, and to help you understand what unconsciously motivates the attitudes and behavior of other people. Each is backed with information about Freud's relevant theories and full explanations of what your results mean about you and your unconscious mind.

A brief biography of Sigmund Freud

Sigismund Schlomo Freud was born on 6 May 1856 in Freiberg, Moravia in what is now Czechoslovakia. In 1860, the family moved to Vienna. Before he qualified as a doctor in 1881 Freud worked in medical research. Between late 1885 and early 1886, he studied the effects of hypnosis under the eminent physician Jean-Martin Charcot in Paris. It was here that he had the insight that if hysterical symptoms of, for example, paralysis and blindness could be induced and removed without the patient's awareness through hypnosis, then maybe all neurotic symptoms have an origin which the patient has forgotten. Although he was later to abandon hypnosis as a method of treatment, it taught him that people are often unaware of (but still influenced by) forgotten memories, and this helped him to formulate his ideas about an unconscious area of the mind (the area of the mind that we're usually unaware of).

Freud opened a private practice in Vienna in 1886, marrying his fiancée, Martha Bernays, in the same year. Using his own methods of "free association" and interpretation, he viewed himself as an archaeologist of the mind, digging into his patients' pasts, unearthing what for years had been buried. His most famous book, *The Interpretation of Dreams*, was published in 1899, though dated 1900. In 1938, after living in Vienna for almost all of his life, Freud was forced to leave Austria because of continuing persecution by the Nazis. He settled at 20 Maresfield Gardens, Hampstead, London with his wife and youngest daughter Anna, and died there at the age of 83 on 23 September 1939.

Freud's legacy
Freud's enduring influence can be seen in the way that most people now take for granted that there is an unconscious area of the mind and accept the idea that what we experience as children influences what we later do as adults. Insight into the unconscious is important because without it we act as puppets with strings pulled by who we were when we were children.

In 1933, the Nazis burned copies of Freud's books in Berlin. However, the complete works of Sigmund Freud are contained within twenty-four volumes and have been translated into many different languages. The names associated with his most celebrated case histories, "Rat Man," "Wolf Man," "Dora," "Judge Schreber," and "Little Hans" are redolent of his consulting room at Bergasse 19 and remain required reading for analysts in training. But Freud didn't only write about his patients, about dreams, and about neurotic symptoms. He wrote, too, about religion, politics, culture, civilization, and the arts, producing a unique view of the world that is neither religious nor scientific. Add to this the multi-million dollar therapy industry that has grown up since Freud and it becomes clear that we live in a very Freudian world.

Freud under analysis

Freud has been criticized for not understanding women, for being out of date, and for not being scientific. Harsh words, particularly as Freud helped women to find their voice—for example, sexually in an era when female sexual desire was hardly acknowledged. He taught psychiatry that neurotic problems can be "cured" psychologically; and, without being scientific, raised the profile of children more than anyone else in the twentieth century. Other criticisms include his generalizing from his patients to the rest of us (arguably preferable to generalizing from the long-suffering laboratory rat); his failure to use scientifically testable hypotheses (arguably better than having a black-and-white view of life); and his design of an expensive and time-consuming therapy (not in itself a criticism of psychoanalytic theory).

To be fair to his critics, Freud's work is unscientific, not least because his conclusions are based on his own subjective analyses of his patients' memories of their childhoods. This makes his psychoanalytic work interpretive rather than predictive. Freud acknowledged this himself, writing in 1922, for example: "The synthesis is thus not so satisfactory as the analysis; in other words, from a knowledge of the premises, we could not have foretold the nature of the result." A more general problem for psychoanalysis is that there is no mechanism within it to get rid of ideas that sound plausible but which turn out to be wrong.

This is partly because psychoanalysts usually have insufficient knowledge of science or research methods to know how to test their ideas rigorously. On the other hand, we don't use experimentation and probability to study literature, art, or music, and equally these methods may not be the best ones to use to understand human nature.

NOW you lie down on the couch . . .

To get as much as you can out of the questionnaires, it is important to answer the questions honestly. To do this, work fairly quickly through each set of questions, without pausing too long over any particular one. Be careful about the wording, though. For example, if a question asks "Do you always. . .?" only answer "Yes" if you really think "always" (rather than "sometimes") applies to you. The same applies to words such as "often," "frequently," "ever," "usually," and "generally." There are no "right" or "wrong" answers, so try not to leave any blanks. If you're really not sure whether to answer "Yes" or "No," give what you think is, on balance, the closest answer. Although each questionnaire contains sufficient questions to give you an accurate overall score, you'll probably disagree with some of the interpretations. That's all right—they won't all fit everybody absolutely perfectly, so you may very occasionally feel that you belong in a different category. It is a good idea, too, to read all the interpretations for each questionnaire because that way you'll be able to compare yourself with other people.

By taking your place on the Freudian couch you are making a decision to travel to the farthest reaches of your unconscious. As you work your way through the questionnaires you will start to see yourself as Freud would have seen you and also to understand how he saw other people. When you get off the couch at the end, you will have developed a Freudian insight into why you do things, and will therefore be a different person.

1 You and Freud

Freud's way of looking at the mind revolutionized how we see ourselves. He showed us that far from being masters of our own destinies we are not even rulers in our own minds. The questionnaires in this section are about your unconscious. The first explores how much insight into your unconscious you already have, the second your motivation to discover more about it.

How much insight do you have?

Do you know why you do things or would you rather not? How aware are you of your unconscious?

		Yes	No
1.	Do you think that some physical diseases can be caused by how a person thinks?	☐	☐
2.	Do you often think about the meaning of life?	☐	☐
3.	Do you sometimes have thoughts that don't really seem to be your own?	☐	☐
4.	Do you always like to have music on in the background?	☐	☐
5.	Are you sometimes surprised by the strength of your reactions to seemingly trivial events?	☐	☐
6.	Do you think that it's more important to be successful than it is to have self-knowledge?	☐	☐
7.	Do you often think about your childhood?	☐	☐
8.	If you can, do you avoid watching a sad movie?	☐	☐
9.	Do you sometimes get anxious for no apparent reason?	☐	☐
10.	If you came across some of your old school reports, would you be interested in looking at them?	☐	☐
11.	Do you sometimes enjoy doing nothing and letting your mind wander?	☐	☐
12.	If you forget to phone a friend, do you ask yourself why you forgot?	☐	☐
13.	Do you think that knowing about the past can help you to predict the future?	☐	☐
14.	Are you, or have you ever been, interested in hypnosis?	☐	☐
15.	If you had an unexpected day off, would you try to keep busy rather than put your feet up?	☐	☐

16. Do you prefer Hollywood movies to "serious" independent films? ☐ ☐
17. Are you interested in what people are all about? ☐ ☐
18. Do you think that celebrity culture is unfairly criticized? ☐ ☐
19. Do you think nostalgia is self-indulgent and stops people getting on with life? ☐ ☐
20. Do you like to live life in the fast lane? ☐ ☐

Interpret your score

Give yourself one point for each answer that matches the key:

1. Yes	5. No	9. No	13. Yes	17. Yes
2. Yes	6. No	10. Yes	14. Yes	18. No
3. No	7. Yes	11. Yes	15. No	19. No
4. No	8. No	12. Yes	16. No	20. No

0–4 Computers don't have an unconscious, don't dream, and don't know why they do things—they're robots. You, on the other hand, do have an unconscious, but you're quite often out of touch with it. Because your insights about yourself are limited (Why this career? Why those friends? Why not that partner?), you may have less control over your life than you think you do.

5–9 At night the moon appears from behind the clouds and then disappears again—a bit like your unconscious. Because you have only fleeting glimpses of your unconscious, you have limited knowledge about yourself—from the moral decisions you make to what you choose to wear. To increase your insight, spend more time reflecting on why you do things; question your motives more.

10–15 Above the entrance to the Temple of Apollo at Delphi were said to be inscribed the words "Know thyself." Sometimes you achieve this goal and gain access to your unconscious, but at other times you have less insight into the decisions you make, whether it's your job, your relationships, or your diet. You are committed to understanding yourself better, though you still sometimes confuse "out of sight" with "out of mind."

16–20 If you were rewarded with air miles for visiting your unconscious you would have earned enough to fly round the world by now. You usually think long and hard about why you do things and, as a result, you have insight into many of the actions you take. You rarely miss an opportunity to learn about yourself and are committed to discovering more.

Insight and the unconscious

Freud's model of the mind has often been likened to an iceberg, and it is as relevant in an age of global warming and melting polar ice-caps as it was when he wrote about it. The tip of the iceberg is our conscious mind and the greater mass submerged beneath the surface is our unconscious mind. Between the conscious and the unconscious, at the visible base of the iceberg, preconscious thoughts and feelings slip in and out of consciousness. Conscious thoughts are what you are aware of at any particular moment, while preconscious thoughts are those things that you can become aware of if you want to—the name of your local supermarket, for example. Unconscious thoughts and feelings, because they involve unexpressed drives, forbidden sexual interests, and other unacknowledged impulses, are more deeply submerged. Freud thought that access to this unconscious area of the mind can give us insight into what it is that motivates us.

Unconscious motives

The Freudian unconscious is not just a trash can waiting to receive our discarded thoughts. On the contrary, Freud viewed the unconscious as a powerful, self-governing mental system, which almost completely without our awareness motivates everything we do. He thought that when we are born the unconscious contains only primitive drives (*triebe* in the original German, though often referred to as instincts), which, as we develop, try to find expression, surfacing as urges and desires, wishes and fantasies—frequently sexual and often aggressive. Since we find these feelings threatening, we try to repress them, but the things we think we have got rid of remain active in our unconscious and continue to exert a powerful influence over the decisions we think we are consciously choosing to make.

Defenses against anxiety

According to Freud, a major source of anxiety arises when feelings that we have disowned threaten, or actually start, to leak up from our unconscious into our conscious mind. To try to prevent this from happening, we use a variety of unconscious strategies or defense mechanisms. An example of an unconscious defense mechanism is when we say we're not angry when, in fact, we're furious—a case of "denial." Freud thought that we deny our anger like this precisely because we are so angry. In other words, we're frightened unconsciously that were we to express our anger it might get out of control. Later, we may "displace" our anger into forgetfulness—we forget, for example, to phone this person that we're "not" angry with. To put it another way, the two events, denying our anger and making the person disappear through our forgetfulness, are invisibly connected in our unconscious mind. Admittedly, this is not easy to prove scientifically.

Finding the unconscious

Freud thought that putting things out of mind is never one hundred percent successful. In particular, he thought that the emotion attached to something we have put out of mind continues to exert an influence over us, which, in some cases, causes us anxiety. In the above example of forgetting to phone the person we are angry with, the experiences we have at one point in the day may lead us to act (or not act, for that matter) in particular ways later in the day. Freud thought that the same thing happens over periods of years. In particular, he thought that the feelings and the passions that we experience as children continue to influence us as adults, even though we may have consciously forgotten about them. Freud viewed this as problematical as it means that we're constantly being influenced by thoughts and feelings that we've put out of mind and are, therefore, unaware of—the disturbing implication of this being that none of us is totally in control of our own mind.

Freud managed to find evidence of the unconscious in just about everything, including our dreams, art, and culture, in what a person reveals in their analytic sessions, through the type of person we are, our psychological problems, everyday accidents (Freudian slips)—even in the jokes that make us laugh. And since he thought that everything we do, whether it's "normal" or "abnormal," is caused by the unconscious, he saw no difference, in principle, between people who are patients and people who are not patients. There is therefore a close relationship in Freud's work between theory and practice, his theories deriving from his work with patients, his consulting room serving as his laboratory.

The next questionnaire is designed to see how many of the qualities that Freud expected those who consulted him to have—whether patients or analysts in training—you have.

Is psychoanalysis for you?

How motivated are you to find out more about yourself? Would you be prepared to make sacrifices to be in analysis?

		Yes	No
1.	Do you set time aside to reflect on why you do things?	☐	☐
2.	Are you someone who likes to leave no stone unturned?	☐	☐
3.	"A problem shared is a problem halved." Do you think this is true?	☐	☐
4.	Would you object to lying on the analytic couch?	☐	☐
5.	Would you object to talking about your dreams?	☐	☐
6.	Would you be prepared to see your analyst more than once a week?	☐	☐
7.	Would you be prepared to see your analyst three times a week?	☐	☐
8.	Would you be prepared to see your analyst five times a week?	☐	☐
9.	Do you think your childhood still influences you?	☐	☐
10.	There are only a few times that your analyst is free to see you. Would you object to seeing your analyst in the mornings before work?	☐	☐
11.	Would you be prepared to see your analyst on a Saturday morning?	☐	☐
12.	A relative of yours is reminiscing about you when you were a child. You can politely leave now or you can stay and listen. Would you stay to find out more?	☐	☐
13.	Would you refuse to make financial economies to afford to remain in analysis?	☐	☐
14.	Would you be prepared to work extra hours to afford to remain in analysis?	☐	☐

15. "Let sleeping dogs lie." Is this a good plan? ☐ ☐
16. Would you be prepared to talk to your analyst ☐ ☐
about your childhood?
17. Would you try to forget about your analysis ☐ ☐
between sessions?
18. Do you think that some things happen "by ☐ ☐
mistake on purpose"?
19. Do you think that it shows weakness to talk about ☐ ☐
your feelings?
20. Do you think that it would be all right to lie to ☐ ☐
your analyst?

Interpret your score

Give yourself one point for each answer that matches the key:

1. Yes	5. No	9. Yes	13. No	17. No
2. Yes	6. Yes	10. No	14. Yes	18. Yes
3. Yes	7. Yes	11. Yes	15. No	19. No
4. No	8. Yes	12. Yes	16. Yes	20. No

0–4 Want to know why you go for that particular type? Why some people irritate you so much? Why you repeat the same mistakes? No? You may want to ask yourself why that is. Maybe someone who doesn't know you very well gave you this book; alternatively, you may have ordered it by mistake or picked up the wrong book at the counter. If none of these applies to you, you may yet surprise yourself.

5–9 Question: how many psychotherapists does it take to change a light bulb? Answer: one, but it's got to want to change. Sound familiar? You would like to know more about yourself but have been somewhat resistant to doing anything about it. Maybe you're a born skeptic or maybe you haven't been ready to change your experience of yourself. Maybe you've been uneasy about what might turn up on the couch.

10–15 Your attitude toward psychoanalysis swings like a compass needle between the North Pole and the South Pole. Some of the time you have a strong conviction about the value of psychoanalysis but at other times you are skeptical. High on motivation but prepared to ask questions: to a bad analyst you would be as welcome as a hungry polar bear; to a good analyst it would be like meeting a fellow explorer.

16–20 Top marks for motivation. You are, in many ways, an ideal candidate for psychoanalysis, committed as you are to finding out more about yourself. Remember that a psychoanalyst is only a person, though. With such high standards, you could find it difficult to find an analyst who can live up to your expectations. Analytic homework: think about where you learnt to expect so much.

How psychoanalysis works

In the same way that the Slow Food movement, founded by Carlo Petrini in Italy in 1986, is concerned with unhurried, traditional methods of farming, food production, and cooking, so the aim of psychoanalysis is to uncover slowly and gradually the causes of a person's problems. As a psychotherapy, psychoanalysis is based on the principle of "psychic determinism." This is the principle that everything we do and feel in the present is influenced by unconscious thoughts and experiences that we have carried forward from the past. Since we are unaware of these influences (because they are unconscious), the aim of psychoanalysis is to make what is unconscious conscious. This way the past should no longer be able, in theory, to influence us without our awareness.

The talking cure

Freud's patients experienced a variety of psychological problems, ranging from phobias and depression to obsessive-compulsive behavior and hysteria. He thought that if they talked freely about their childhoods the cause of their problems would come to the surface and they would be relieved of their symptoms. He saw patients/analysands (those training to become psychoanalysts) sometimes five or even six times a week, so commitment and motivation were important. Each day, there was time set aside (nowadays known as the "fifty-minute hour") that belonged exclusively to the person he was seeing—whether or not they kept their appointment. During these daily sessions the patient would lie on the analytic couch in Freud's consulting room while Freud would sit at the head of the couch, listening with "evenly suspended attention" (attentively and without interruption) to what the person said. The idea of a "talking cure" is said to have originated with Bertha Pappenheim, known as Anna O, a patient of Joseph Breuer, an early collaborator of Freud, who referred to it as "chimney sweeping."

Revealing the unconscious

In these daily sessions, Freud used three principal methods to uncover what was going on in the patient's unconscious. The first method was "free association" (*freier Einfall*, or "free irruption," in the original German), which means, in practice, letting one idea follow another. To do this, the patient follows the "basic rule" of psychoanalysis, which is that no matter how embarrassing it may be or how trivial it may seem, you say aloud whatever comes to mind without allowing your conscious mind to censor your unconscious thoughts.

The second method was dream interpretation. In the belief that dreams are created in our unconscious mind, Freud encouraged his patients to report any dreams or fragments of dreams that they had had since the previous day. His patients would then make whatever associations they could to the dream (what did the dream make them think of or feel, in other words) and Freud would interpret these associations with the patient.

Freud's third method was to interpret the relationship that the patient developed toward him (the so-called "transference relationship"). Freud thought that how patients treated him was a replay (now unconscious) of ways they had learnt to respond in their family and at school. This revealed, in turn, how, for unconscious reasons, patients currently dealt with other people in their life (passively, competitively, dependently, and so forth).

Freud's view of therapy

Freud never promised to eliminate psychological distress altogether. He suggested only that it might be possible to transform "hysterical misery into common unhappiness." On the face of it, this may seem pessimistic, but it is also realistic. Aware that we cannot always express our instincts as we might wish to within society, Freud hoped that psychoanalysis would help us to understand this predicament better and so find more constructive, less self-deceptive ways of dealing with it.

The fact that psychoanalysis (Freudian or otherwise) costs so much time and money doesn't make psychoanalytic theory wrong. On the other hand, when a person invests time and money on themselves, they're likely to be motivated to see things differently. When we spend a lot of money on something, we usually want to convince ourselves that it was a good decision to do so—in this case, believing that you feel better could be a way of justifying the outlay. Change may occur, too, as a result of the relationship between the patient/analysand and their analyst—people may like themselves better because they have been accepted for the person they are.

Freud's discovery of a method of investigating the unconscious was one of his great achievements. The next section explores how he conceptualized the structure of your mind and why your mind sometimes seems to be in conflict with itself.

2 Your Freudian personality

The questionnaires in this section are based on Freud's tripartite division of the mind into the "id," the "ego," and the "superego." The first considers the extent to which your id compels you to gratify your instincts, the second measures the strength of your ego, the third explores the type of superego or conscience you have.

Who's in control of your id?

Can you resist temptation or are you a slave to your instincts? Do you act on impulse or are you always in control?

		Yes	No
1.	When you go shopping, do you sometimes return home with items that you didn't intend to buy?	☐	☐
2.	Do you find waiting in line easy?	☐	☐
3.	Do you eat at fast food restaurants more than three times a week?	☐	☐
4.	At a theme park, do you like to go on the rides that produce the most adrenaline?	☐	☐
5.	It's late at night. There's someone bingeing in front of the fridge. Could this be you?	☐	☐
6.	You're at a bus stop. Thirty minutes later you're still there. If you had the cash, would you hail a passing cab?	☐	☐
7.	Do you have more than five tattoos and/or body piercings in total?	☐	☐
8.	Do you have any genital piercings?	☐	☐
9.	Are you prone to doing things that you later regret?	☐	☐
10.	Do you feel guilty if you indulge yourself?	☐	☐
11.	A hedonist is devoted to the pursuit of pleasure and happiness as a way of life. Are you?	☐	☐
12.	Do you regularly make an effort to buy wholesome, organic food?	☐	☐
13.	Do you try to avoid unusual experiences?	☐	☐
14.	If you were in a casino and you'd used up your budget, would you leave rather than buy more chips?	☐	☐
15.	Do you like to switch TV channels frequently?	☐	☐
16.	Do you enjoy scary movies?	☐	☐

17. Do you generally put the needs of other people ☐ ☐ before your needs?
18. Does being a member of a club for dangerous ☐ ☐ sports appeal to you?
19. Have you ever used a recreational drug—for ☐ ☐ example marijuana or ecstasy?
20. Do you often worry about doing the "wrong" ☐ ☐ thing?

Interpret your score

Give yourself one point for each answer that matches the key:

1. Yes	5. Yes	9. Yes	13. No	17. No
2. No	6. Yes	10. No	14. No	18. Yes
3. Yes	7. Yes	11. Yes	15. Yes	19. Yes
4. Yes	8. Yes	12. No	16. Yes	20. No

0–4 You currently find it hard to give up even a fraction of control over your id. You seem to think that there's something wrong with gratifying your instincts, that if you do so you should feel guilty, that being impulsive will make you a slave to your desires. Remember the saying, "A little of what you fancy does you good"? Now's the time to see if it's true.

5–10 Sex, drugs, and rock and roll? Not one hundred percent in your case (perhaps a wise decision) as you are more than capable of exerting control over your id. It's not that you don't ever act on impulse or take a chance, but it's you who decides when, where, and how often. You have, in short, red-blooded instincts coursing through your veins and are capable of holding them in check.

11–16 As much at ease with the devoutly religious as with a fellow clubber, you are neither a party pooper nor a slave to your instinctual urges—rather, you are a past master at controlling your id while at the same time not imposing too many restrictions on yourself. You have no trouble gratifying your instincts but can take your foot off the gas when you need to.

17–20 You don't appear to have much control over your id. You are in thrall to the "pleasure principle" and care mostly about satisfying your own needs. You seem to have little ability (or maybe no desire) to delay your gratification, either in your own interest or anyone else's. Some people might be envious of your self-indulgence; others would accuse you of being irresponsible.

In the beginning was the id

In an achievement-oriented, me, me, me Western culture in which market forces encourage the survival of the fittest, the "id," the Latin word for "it" (*das Es*, or "the It," in the original German) plays the same part in making a killing on the financial markets as it does in finding lunch on the African savanna. The id is part of Freud's structural model of the mind. He argued that the relationship between the id (our animal drives), the ego (our rational self), and the superego (our conscience) makes up our personality. Each part fights for control of our mind and each has the capacity at different times to be either unconscious or conscious—we can either be unaware or aware of its influence over our actions.

The biological imperative

According to Freud, the id is the oldest, most primitive part of our mind—the original source of our instinctual energy or "libido." Freud described the id as a seething mass of biological drives directed toward satisfying our needs for things such as food, warmth, and sex—a dark chaotic area of the mind, driven by what he called the "pleasure principle." The pleasure principle refers to the way in which the id searches for immediate gratification (to avoid "unpleasure") irrespective of the consequences. In this sense, the id is the "spoiled child" of our personality, going to any lengths to satisfy itself. Freud's id is irrational and amoral, unprincipled and anarchic; if the id believes in anything, it believes in itself.

How the id thinks

The way in which the id thinks is not rational: Freud called it "primary process" thinking. Primary process thinking lies behind our fantasies and our dreams, taking no account of space or time as we experience them in the everyday world. This is why you are free in your dreams to have unreal experiences, to be with whom you want, to travel in time, to be in any place your unconscious wishes.

Satisfying the id

From the id's point of view, outlets for its expression should ideally be real. Since this is often prohibited, we also express the id indirectly in fantasy and imagination. Freud thought, too, that fantasies are the precursors of thoughts. By this he meant that when we were infants the development of the ability to imagine what we wanted—the breast or the bottle, for example—was an early form of thinking. People gratify their instincts by watching others indulge them, too: spectator sports, the circus, horror movies, and pornography all offer vicarious thrills to the id.

Since our id, or infant self, is so irresponsible, civilization makes sure that we keep this side of our personality under wraps. The pressure exerted by the id to resurface in feelings we no longer recognize as our own can then become a source of anxiety. In everyday life, people generally redirect their id's libidinal energy along "respectable" cultural pathways—sport,

the arts, entertainment, and so on—in a process known as "sublimation," described later on.

Instincts and relationships

Freud's portrayal of a conflict between our id, ego, and superego
is intuitively appealing because by naming parts of the mind he
made it sound as if they exist in the real world. It also reflects the
dilemma we all face of how to express our instincts while not
transgressing society's rules. Having trained as a neurologist, he
would probably have been delighted to learn that there are areas
of the brain now known to be involved in aggression and
emotion and others that inhibit their expression. Not that all
contemporary psychoanalysts and psychotherapists subscribe to
the idea that we have powerful instinctual drives that need to be
controlled in the way that Freud described. Some theorists, for
example, prefer to think that we have a basic drive to form
relationships with other people rather than an underlying drive
to be aggressive or sexual. For them, aggression comes about as a
consequence of being frustrated and sexuality serves as an
expression of intimacy.

From a Freudian point of view, a person who is all id is, in theory,
a psychopath. The next questionnaire is therefore about the part
of the mind that moderates the id—namely, the ego.

How strong is your ego?

Do you live in the real world or do you live in a world of fantasy?
Are you ruled by your head or by your heart?

		Yes	No
1.	Are you good at making decisions?	☐	☐
2.	Do you pride yourself on how logical you are?	☐	☐
3.	Do everyday events in your life tend to overwhelm you?	☐	☐
4.	Do you try hard to keep your bank account in credit?	☐	☐
5.	Do you know what your correct body weight should be?	☐	☐
6.	Are there any bad habits or addictions that you've been unable to give up?	☐	☐
7.	Do you usually have your feet on the ground?	☐	☐
8.	Do you ever worry that people are going to find out that you're not as competent as they think you are?	☐	☐
9.	Do you mind if other people make your decisions for you?	☐	☐
10.	You really want to see a new movie. A newspaper critic trashes it. Do you still go and see it?	☐	☐
11.	Are you the kind of person who takes control in an emergency?	☐	☐
12.	Do you favor intuition over logic when solving problems?	☐	☐
13.	Would you ever change a decision you had already made because of what a horoscope predicted?	☐	☐
14.	Are you prepared to take a stand over something with which everyone else disagrees?	☐	☐
15.	Do you believe in the supernatural?	☐	☐

16. Do you have a strong sense of who you are, where you came from, and where you're going? ☐ ☐
17. Do you avoid taking responsibility for what you do? ☐ ☐
18. If you undertake to do something, are you usually confident you will be successful? ☐ ☐
19. Do you generally get things right the first time? ☐ ☐
20. Do you often feel very vulnerable? ☐ ☐

Interpret your score

Give yourself one point for each answer that matches the key:

1. Yes	5. Yes	9. Yes	13. No	17. No
2. Yes	6. No	10. Yes	14. Yes	18. Yes
3. No	7. Yes	11. Yes	15. No	19. Yes
4. Yes	8. No	12. No	16. Yes	20. No

0–4 You and your ego appear to be in the middle of an identity crisis. At times you find it hard to make even the simplest of decisions or to commit yourself to anything, preferring to dither rather than to make up your mind. Until you can be more consistently decisive, don't apply for executive positions requiring leadership or decision-making skills. Ego strength 3 out of 10.

5–10 Eccentric American chess genius Bobby Fischer took the world by storm in 1972 when he defeated Boris Spassky of the Soviet Union in Reykjavik, Iceland to become world champion. You don't have to be a grandmaster to enjoy a game of chess, but neither do you need to be as emotional about it as he was. To maximize your ego's potential, keep a check on the amount of superstitious thinking you do. Ego strength 5 out of 10.

11–16 The six layers of your neocortex—the most recently evolved part of the brain, with which you do your thinking—are usually in control of the emotional centers in your brain. Your sense of identity is only occasionally in doubt and your strong ego and no-nonsense approach to life ensure that you are decisive when you need to be. Ego strength 7 out of 10.

17–20 You have an ultra strong ego. You are probably an admirer of Mr. Spock in *Startrek*, as you invariably think logically and your decisions are nearly always rational. You are almost never superstitious and can't understand people who are. Since you are not from the planet Vulcan, make sure that you don't miss out on the emotional side of life. Ego strength 10 out of 10.

The ego—in touch with reality

The difference between having a big Mac and having a big ego lies in the nature of the inflation: physical in the first case, psychological in the second. Not that this is what Freud had in mind when he—or, that is to say, his translators—used the word "ego," the Latin word for "I" (*das Ich*, or "the I," in the original German) to describe the executive, decision-making part of our personality. It is our ego, he argued, that has to keep a balance between the biological drives of the id and the moral restrictions of the superego. As well as having to resolve these internal tensions between our instincts and our conscience, the ego is also the part of us that relates to the outside world.

How the ego thinks

In order to carry out these functions, the ego uses what Freud called "secondary process" thinking. Contrary to the fantasy-driven primary process thinking of the id, secondary process thinking is rational and logical. The ego therefore works according to the "reality principle," meaning that it takes account of the real world when making decisions. If, for example, we're tempted to overeat or we're about to lose our temper, or if our id is excited by a sexually attractive stranger, it is our ego that prevents us from acting out our feelings too impulsively. This is not because our ego is particularly scrupulous, but because it is governed by the reality principle. Freud likened the relationship between the id and the ego to that of a horse and its rider. The ego only relaxes its control when we are asleep, so allowing the id free rein in our dreams.

The development of self-awareness

Freud believed that we are born without an ego. Our ego, he argued, develops out of the id. This happens as we discover through the experience of our senses that there is a difference between what is "me" and what is "not me." Gradually, as this happens, the ego takes up a position between the outside world and our own inner world and we develop self-awareness.

The ego is the vulnerable part of our personality, protecting itself from id impulses and from feelings of guilt originating in the superego by trying to forget about things or repress them. When this does not work, it is our ego that feels overwhelmed and it is the ego's unconscious defense mechanisms that are used to counteract anxiety. The ego, or at least a part of it, is also the part of a person that forms a "therapeutic alliance" with their analyst; over the course of an analysis, it is the ego that is strengthened.

Freud wrote in 1933: "Where id was, there shall ego be." By this he meant that only when something that is unconscious has been recalled, made conscious, and worked through by the ego can it cease to influence us unconsciously. Or, to paraphrase his admirer David Stafford-Clark, what we cannot remember we cannot leave behind; in other words, we can only truly forget what our ego has remembered.

The next questionnaire is about your conscience or superego. As well as keeping your id under control, the ego has to make sure that your superego isn't working overtime.

Do you have a guilty conscience?

Do you sleep the sleep of the just? Or are you troubled by what Freud called your superego?

		Yes	No
1.	Do you behave differently when you know you're on CCTV?	☐	☐
2.	Would you make a false declaration on a tax form?	☐	☐
3.	Have you ever taken a day off sick when you weren't sick?	☐	☐
4.	Would you find it easy to write yourself a glowing reference?	☐	☐
5.	Do you feel guilty if you walk straight past someone begging in the street?	☐	☐
6.	Do you often feel ashamed of yourself?	☐	☐
7.	Does seeing a policeman make you feel guilty?	☐	☐
8.	Do you set yourself very high standards?	☐	☐
9.	Do you criticize yourself more than other people criticize you?	☐	☐
10.	If you were to mentally undress someone you found sexually attractive, would it make you feel guilty?	☐	☐
11.	Do you think that telling a white lie is OK?	☐	☐
12.	Does it take much to make you feel conscience-stricken?	☐	☐
13.	Do you often tell yourself what a good person you are?	☐	☐
14.	Do you generally try to placate other people?	☐	☐
15.	You catch a train at the last minute, without a ticket. There is no one to collect the fare at your destination. Would you consider posting the money to the rail company?	☐	☐

16. Are you sometimes "economical" with the truth? ☐ ☐
17. Are you comfortable if you don't recycle as much household waste as you can? ☐ ☐
18. Do you sometimes hate yourself? ☐ ☐
19. Are you a bit of a prude? ☐ ☐
20. Do you sleep in at weekends if you have the opportunity to do so? ☐ ☐

Interpret your score

Give yourself one point for each answer that matches the key:

1. Yes	5. Yes	9. Yes	13. No	17. No
2. No	6. Yes	10. Yes	14. Yes	18. Yes
3. No	7. Yes	11. No	15. Yes	19. Yes
4. No	8. Yes	12. No	16. No	20. No

0–4 Like a Mafia godfather, you claim that if you don't look after Number One no one else is going to and that there's no point in having a guilty conscience about it. Maybe you felt hard done by as a child or maybe you're reacting against having been made to feel guilty. Maybe you were overindulged. Whatever it was, you're not troubled excessively by your superego.

5–10 Inside every saint there's a sinner trying to get out. This isn't meant to fudge the issue but to make it clear that, in your case, although your superego doesn't always make it easy for you to be a sinner, you're not a total puritan either. Although you developed a reasonably clear conscience in childhood, you still feel guilty when you break the rules.

11–16 You have the type of superego that makes you feel guilty at least once a week. Some people would say it's just the kind of person you are; others would say it's the way you were brought up. It's probably a combination of factors. Because it's hard to live up to such expectations, your self-esteem is sometimes dented. Set yourself more achievable goals and you will be able to praise yourself more often.

17–20 While some people have an overactive thyroid, you may have an overactive superego. This is why you find it so difficult to enjoy yourself or to let yourself go. While it could be, in part, that you were born that way, you may have been set (or maybe you set them for yourself) excessively high standards as a child. To feel less guilty, aim to be more realistic and think about your good points more often. Stop being so hard on yourself.

Superego—origin of a guilty conscience?

The word "superego" (*das Uber-Ich*, or "the Above-I," in the original German) sounds a bit like the name of a dessert, a pavlova, say—a gigantic meringue topped with whipped cream and raspberries. The truth is quite the opposite: its role in our life is not to encourage gratification but to inhibit indulgence. So, while the id is the source of our biological drives and the ego contains our common sense, our superego is the site of our moral values and our conscience.

Where the superego comes from
According to Freud, the superego is formed through our early experiences with our parents or other caregivers whose values we absorb, or identify with, as though they are our own. As we grow older, we identify with other people, such as teachers and relatives, who we also both admire and fear. Gradually, we acquire the cultural values of a superego that in time we will pass down to future generations.

The superego can be divided into two parts: conscience and "ego-ideal." Our conscience is an internalized "punishing parent" who criticizes and prohibits "bad" behavior and makes us feel guilty by threatening us with punishment. Our ego-ideal is an internalized "rewarding parent" who praises us for our "good" behavior and raises our self-esteem.

How the superego develops

Freud dated the development of the superego to within what is known as the "phallic" stage of development when we are between about three and five or six years of age. This stage of development was said by Freud to be characterized by heightened awareness of genital differences between the sexes and to be when "Oedipal" rivalries with the same-sex parent are first played out.

Freud concluded, controversially, that anatomical differences between the sexes result in boys and girls developing different types of conscience. A superego derived from a fear of losing your mother's love, as is the case for girls, will lead to a less authoritarian type of conscience (unhappily he suggested morally inferior) than one created in the shadow of the fear of castration, as is the case for boys.

Punishing ourselves

Anatomical differences aside, there is another question that affects us all, which is how we can account for the fact that our own conscience may be harsher than anything our parents would wish for us. One explanation is that since the superego is formed from the raw material of the id it contains elements of the id's irrationality, which sometimes makes our conscience irrationally harsh. Freud thought, too, that any of our own hostility and rage that we are unable to express gets recirculated and absorbed, in part, by our superego. Both these factors would make our conscience less of a parental clone and more a product of our own making.

How the id, ego, and superego relate to one another is determined, in part, during "psychosexual development." Freudian psychosexual theory argues that as we become progressively aware of different parts of our body during childhood so our mind develops in corresponding stages, and this is what the next section is about.

3 The Freudian child

The questionnaires in this section are based on the stages of a child's development that Freud described. Freudians believe that if we have too much or too little pleasure at any of the stages we can get stuck there and that this will show up in later life.

Do you have an oral personality?

Freud noticed that some of us have more of a love affair with our mouth than others. How much do you enjoy using yours?

		Yes	No
1.	Do you regard food as one of the great pleasures of life?	☐	☐
2.	Do you easily become addicted to things?	☐	☐
3.	Do you know the calorific value of most of the foods you eat?	☐	☐
4.	If a scientist invented a pill that took the place of food, would you be at the head of the line for it?	☐	☐
5.	Did you suck your thumb as a child?	☐	☐
6.	Do you sometimes eat just to make yourself feel better?	☐	☐
7.	Are you fastidious about eating healthy foods?	☐	☐
8.	Do you still enjoy certain childhood foods?	☐	☐
9.	Would you describe yourself as a pessimist?	☐	☐
10.	Do you think that people should eat whenever they feel like it?	☐	☐
11.	Have you ever compulsively overeaten?	☐	☐
12.	Do you consider carefully the nutritional value of all the foods you eat?	☐	☐
13.	Have you ever starved yourself on purpose?	☐	☐
14.	Are you an extremely independent person?	☐	☐
15.	Do you think that desserts are an unnecessary indulgence that people could well do without?	☐	☐
16.	Could you tell the difference between a strawberry and raspberry yogurt with your eyes closed?	☐	☐
17.	Do you enjoy snacking between meals?	☐	☐
18.	Do you have a preference for oral sex?	☐	☐
19.	If you go on a diet, are you capable of sticking to it?	☐	☐
20.	Do you have a tendency toward bingeing?	☐	☐

Interpret your score

Give yourself one point for each answer that matches the key:

1. Yes	5. Yes	9. No	13. No	17. Yes
2. Yes	6. Yes	10. Yes	14. No	18. Yes
3. No	7. No	11. Yes	15. No	19. No
4. No	8. Yes	12. No	16. Yes	20. Yes

0–5 By some people's standards you find oral pleasures such as eating and drinking more of a necessity than a pleasure—compared to them you eat to live rather than live to eat. That doesn't mean that you're not capable of indulging yourself occasionally, but you don't consume enough calories to be accused of having an oral personality.

6–10 You don't enjoy yourself with your mouth as much as some people do and you purse your lips disapprovingly when you see other people overindulging themselves. However, if all the restaurants in the world were to close tomorrow, you'd not only miss the company, you'd also miss the food. Nevertheless, having an oral personality is not something you need to worry about.

11–15 Comfort eat? Yes, you do. But that doesn't mean that you have an oral personality. Find it difficult to stick to a sensible diet? You're not alone. Overindulge? Yes, you do. But you are also capable of showing restraint. All good, because the world can be a cold and unforgiving place and giving yourself treats is a way of looking after yourself.

16–20 As far as you're concerned, your mouth is at times a Michelin three-star restaurant. You have your own regular table, the waiters all know you and solicitously look after your every gustatory need. If you had to give up one of your senses, it wouldn't be the one associated with your mouth—you depend on it too much as a source of pleasure.

Leftovers from the oral stage

In an age of anorexia and bulimia, size zero and morbid obesity, what Freud wrote about the relationship we have with our mouth is as topical as ever. The oral personality type is based on his description of an "oral" stage of development, from birth to about one year old. He noted how as babies we derive intense pleasure first from sucking and then from biting with our mouth, lips, and gums. In the earlier sucking phase (0–6 months) we made discoveries about the world by putting anything we came across (fist, blanket, rattle) in our mouth and sucking on it—the first thing we encountered being the breast or the teat on a feeding bottle. In the later biting phase (6 months plus), with sharp milk teeth coming through, sucking turned to biting and to chewing. This is why the earlier sucking phase is sometimes called "oral passive" while the later biting phase is sometimes referred to as "oral aggressive" or "oral sadistic."

Psychosexual theory

The oral stage is the first of the so-called psychosexual stages. Starting with his *Three Essays on the Theory of Sexuality* (1905), Freud charted our childhood psychological development as a sequence of stages, each stage ("oral," "anal," "phallic," and "genital") named after a part of the body. Freud used the word "sexual" in a very wide sense in this context to include all ecstatic, sensual pleasures, picturing the newborn baby as "polymorphously perverse." By this he meant that we are capable of deriving intense pleasure from any zone of the body (potentially with different objects, too) and that these parts of our body later become erogenous zones.

Adult orality

Freudians claim that traces of the oral stage persist in activities as diverse as kissing, swearing, chewing gum, and pen sucking. The earlier sucking phase is associated with oral habits such as thumb sucking, overeating, smoking, and heavy drinking, as well as with non-oral dependencies and addictions. In contrast, oral sadism may show up in a tendency to be verbally abusive (mouthing off) or to use biting sarcasm and, through a process of reversal, biting your nails. In addition to speculation that a sexual proclivity for fellatio and cunnilingus might originate at the oral stage, it has been suggested that dentists may unconsciously choose to spend their entire professional lives looking into other people's mouths for the same reason. Others who use their own mouths to earn a living include restaurant critics, singers, and wind instrumentalists, who exquisitely adapt their lips to fit the orifice of their chosen instrument. An arcane oral interpretation of anorexia nervosa (in girls) has it that eating is symbolic of sex and so induces feelings of guilt, and that becoming fat is symbolically equated with pregnancy.

Oral personality characteristics

In a light-hearted review of the implications of Freudian psycho-sexual theory, the psychologist Paul Kline reflected that, in addition to the sucking and biting side of things, how we were actually fed during the oral stage will show up in the kind of person we are, and even in our national character. If we were fed according to a strict timetable (scheduled feeding), we may be tight-lipped and disapproving of any oral laxity or overindulgence. If, on the other hand, we were fed whenever we wanted to be fed (demand feeding), we may be uninhibited about eating and drinking. A similar argument underlies the idea that optimists are created by prolonged breast- or bottle-feeding while early weaning produces pessimists. The French national character, because of its association with a love of food and wine, is therefore described as an oral one; in the same way, an excess of early oral satisfaction could have something to do with why so many in the West are overweight. It doesn't necessarily follow that each time you go to the fridge to get milk you're unconsciously thinking of your mother. On the other hand, a preference in men for women with either small or large breasts is, in theory, traceable to early oral experiences; but then so, too, is Count Dracula's predilection for biting.

Oral analysis

Freud's account of orality doesn't explain the mechanism by which oral memories get carried forward from childhood to adulthood, and the idea that both too much and too little satisfaction can result in a fixation makes the theory difficult to prove or disprove. There may be other reasons for oral overindulgence, too — for instance, some people may have a genetic predisposition to become addicted to cigarettes or alcohol. Neither does the theory explain why one person becomes addicted to one thing and another person to something else. Polymorphous perversity may have an exotic ring to it, but other psychologists have demonstrated, without reference to the unconscious, that anything can become associated with anything. Not that these observations mean that Freud was wrong. Early satisfactions and frustrations at the breast may play a part in shaping our adult inclinations, although when challenged about his own cigar smoking Freud is supposed to have said: "Sometimes a cigar is just a cigar."

If you don't have an oral personality, you could have an anal personality. The next questionnaire moves to the other end of the alimentary canal and measures how far your personality was shaped by your experiences of potty training.

Do you have an anal personality?

How far are your current ways of thinking influenced by your experiences of toilet training? Are you up-tight and ultra-fastidious or are you easygoing and laid-back?

		Yes	No
1.	Are you a person who likes to make lists?	☐	☐
2.	If you won a really large lottery prize, would you give away some of your winnings?	☐	☐
3.	Do you abhor all forms of waste?	☐	☐
4.	Do you enjoy trying out new cleaning products?	☐	☐
5.	Are you capable of being very obstinate?	☐	☐
6.	Can you fully relax when you're not one hundred percent in control?	☐	☐
7.	Are you more often late for appointments than on time?	☐	☐
8.	Does the idea of owning a safe deposit box appeal to you?	☐	☐
9.	Would you rather complete a job imperfectly than leave it unfinished?	☐	☐
10.	You go to see a movie. You arrive just as it's beginning. Do you leave at the end of the movie feeling that you've missed something?	☐	☐
11.	Do you find it easy to let yourself go?	☐	☐
12.	Are you a person who pays a lot of attention to detail?	☐	☐
13.	Do you have an extra sensitive nose when it comes to bad smells?	☐	☐
14.	Do you think people who are very untidy are also untrustworthy?	☐	☐
15.	Are you generous when buying presents?	☐	☐
16.	Do you wear, or would you like to wear, disposable gloves when refueling your car?	☐	☐

17. Do you prefer not to think about bodily functions? ☐ ☐

18. Are you more hygienic than most people you know? ☐ ☐

19. Are you an obsessional kind of person? ☐ ☐

20. Do you enjoy living in a mess? ☐ ☐

Interpret your score

Give yourself one point for each answer that matches the key:

1. Yes	5. Yes	9. No	13. Yes	17. Yes
2. No	6. No	10. Yes	14. Yes	18. Yes
3. Yes	7. No	11. No	15. No	19. Yes
4. Yes	8. Yes	12. Yes	16. Yes	20. No

17–20 You don't necessarily wrinkle up your nose as if there's a bad smell about (Freud's associate Karl Abraham claimed that some anal personality types do this). Neither do you believe that cleanliness is next to godliness, though you can be rather fussy. Try not to go any further in this direction—unless you're aiming to win an award for your anal characteristics.

11–16 You are the kind of person who would happily lend money to a friend, if you had it, but you might also worry about when it was going to be repaid. Since you have easygoing and generous characteristics, as well as mean and fastidious ones, you're not anal enough even to show up in the ratings for "Anal Personality of the Year."

5–10 When people visit you it's generally a good experience for them as the atmosphere is usually relaxed, you're easygoing, and the place is reasonably clean and tidy. This is because you combine qualities of the anal personality type with their exact opposites: tidy and untidy, mean and generous, obstinate and easygoing. A good combination.

0–4 You have almost none of the characteristics of the anal personality type. To people who like less clutter this can be irritating, but to more bohemian types it's chilled. It's not that you're messy exactly—more a matter of being untidy sometimes. And it doesn't mean that you're not capable of being organized. The good thing about not having an anal personality is that people find you generous and kindhearted.

Residues of the anal stage

The marketing and sale of long, plump rolls of extra soft, extra strong toilet tissue is big business today. Nevertheless, maybe because it provokes an uncontrollable visceral response to protect us against disease, anything to do with poop continues to arouse the same strong feelings that it did when Freud wrote about it. The anal personality type is derived from his description of an "anal" stage of development, between about one and three years of age. Anal functions involve the relief and satisfaction of passing a motion (expulsion) and the pleasure in delaying the actual moment of evacuation (retention). Up to now, we did what we had to do as and when it pleased us, but from this point on we were urged by those who looked after us to use a potty and lavishly praised when we did so. Although we will have done what was expected of us some of the time, at other times we will have refused to perform to order, asserting our newfound independence and control.

The anal personality type

As with the other psychosexual stages, Freud thought that the experiences of toilet training are reflected in our adult behavior. If the experiences of potty training are happy and creative, the outcome will be a positive one. This is not the case with the anal personality type. "Anal expulsives," for example, are said to be obsessed with cleanliness, unusually neat and tidy, and preoccupied with punctuality and routines, characteristics interpreted as an unconscious reaction against doing what they'd really like to be doing (I'll show them how clean I can be!). "Anal retentives," on the other hand, are said to be miserly (tight-assed), obstinate, and given to collecting and hoarding things, characteristics interpreted as a continuing attempt from childhood to defy those who trained them (See if they can make me do it!).

Rolling in it

Following Freud's example, it is not uncommon for Freudian psychoanalysts to make an equation between feces and money. This is based on the premise that feces are valuable as far as the child is concerned: to give them up is to give something special — a kind of precious gift. The relationship between money and feces is therefore said to be reflected in expressions such as filthy rich, stinking rich, pouring money down the drain, and making a pile. According to Paul Kline, the Swiss national character, associated as it is with gold, banking, clean streets, and precision timepieces (to which could be added the hygienic manufacture of carefully wrapped chocolate), veers toward the anal. Of course, an alternative, less symbolic, reason why money is considered dirty is that it's handled by people whose hygiene is unknown to us.

Anal expressions

For more tactile reasons, activities such as painting, pottery, and bread-making can be interpreted as substitutes for a childlike interest in playing with feces. This is because they allow us to use our hands and make a mess — mixing, smearing, squelching, and kneading sticky substances. Those at the other end of the anal spectrum may therefore display the opposite characteristics: messy, easygoing, untidy, and generous. No over-control here!

The anal stage has been used by psychoanalysts to interpret obsessions and phobias about dirt, contamination, and germs, which they claim may turn out to be smokescreens for their opposite: an interest in and an excitement about anal and urethral functions. Such ideas may seem "unspeakable" to the person concerned, but to the Freudian analyst they are common currency.

Anal analysis

As with the oral personality type, it is not clear by what mechanism anal memories get carried forward from childhood to adulthood and, once again, having an anal personality could be genetic or caused by experiences other than those of toilet training. Freud's theory is further weakened by the fact that obsessive-compulsive disorder (OCD), which has been associated with the anal stage, can be treated effectively with non-psychoanalytic methods. The reason that Freud's description of this personality type is so accurate may be because he tended toward it himself, rigidly controlling the people he worked with, avidly collecting antiquities, over-generalizing to the point that ideas became doctrine, and obsessively smoking cigars. Luckily, he didn't inhibit artists such as the paint-splattering Jackson Pollock or the spin-painting Damien Hirst; and, as far as collecting and hoarding are concerned, consider that in 2006 the art collector Ronald Lauder paid $135 million for Gustav Klimt's golden portrait of Adele Bloch-Bauer, only for Pollock's painting *No. 5, 1948* to achieve $140 million in November the same year.

In case you're not one hundred percent orally or anally fixated, the next questionnaire investigates arrested development at the phallic stage. Freud traced the self-involvement of a person fixated at this stage to the discovery in childhood of their genitals.

How phallic-minded are you?

Are you concerned about keeping up appearances? Do you enjoy exercising power over other people? How important is status to you?

		Yes	No
1.	Would you say that you're a very ambitious person?	☐	☐
2.	Do you like to own expensive things?	☐	☐
3.	If you were given free access to a fashionable club or gym, would this be good news to you?	☐	☐
4.	If money and pollution were of no importance, would you like to drive a very expensive car?	☐	☐
5.	Do you enjoy looking at pornography?	☐	☐
6.	In a restaurant you have a choice between an expensive and a less expensive bottle of wine. Since you have a cold, you won't be able to tell the difference. Do you choose the less expensive one?	☐	☐
7.	Do you think it's important to gratify yourself sexually with your partner even if your partner doesn't enjoy it?	☐	☐
8.	Is it better to lose graciously than to win ungraciously?	☐	☐
9.	Does the idea of being a celebrity appeal to you?	☐	☐
10.	Do you think it's misguided to be socially ambitious?	☐	☐
11.	Do you enjoy being sexually provocative?	☐	☐
12.	"Variety is the spice of life." Do you think that's true of sex?	☐	☐
13.	Caring for the other person is one of the most rewarding aspects of a relationship. Do you agree with this statement?	☐	☐
14.	Do you regard modesty as a virtue?	☐	☐

15. Sex cannot be a satisfactory end in itself. True? ☐ ☐
16. Do you ever take pleasure in exploiting other people's weaknesses? ☐ ☐
17. "If you've got it, flaunt it." Agree? ☐ ☐
18. Does being a voyeur appeal to you? ☐ ☐
19. Across the street they forget to close the bedroom curtains when getting ready for bed. Would you be tempted to watch? ☐ ☐
20. Do you prefer to socialize with people who are as well or better off than you are? ☐ ☐

Interpret your score

Give yourself one point for each answer that matches the key:

1. Yes	5. Yes	9. Yes	13. No	17. Yes
2. Yes	6. No	10. No	14. No	18. Yes
3. Yes	7. Yes	11. Yes	15. No	19. Yes
4. Yes	8. No	12. Yes	16. Yes	20. Yes

0–4 You are hardly at all phallic-minded, but that doesn't mean that you're not concerned about status. It's not inverted snobbery either—you don't, for example, purposely choose less expensive things in order to demonstrate what you could afford to buy if you wanted to. No. Your answers read almost like a manifesto against what Freud's phallic stage represents.

5–10 Not for you exclusively jewelry from Tiffany & Co., provisions from Fortnum & Mason, or accessories by Gucci. You like to keep up appearances, but you don't depend on status symbols. Exercising power has its moments, but you don't need to take advantage of other people in order to feel good about yourself. Phallic-minded? Occasionally.

11–16 Collecting the odd status symbol and taking advantage of other people occasionally may work reasonably well to raise your self-esteem, but underneath you remain as vulnerable as the next person. So the question you should be asking yourself is not should I buy this or should I buy that, but why do I feel the need to buy it? Phallic-minded? Some of the time.

17–20 Phallic-minded? The word that comes to mind is tumescent. You have, at times, an engorged and swollen quest for power that leaves little to the imagination. You collect status symbols like there's no tomorrow. Why the need? Who to impress? Your obsession with appearances is like an addiction.

Phallic fixations

In nature, the link between status and reproduction is universal: fast cars, a fat bank account, and expensive clothes are the equivalent of the glamorous, iridescent peacock's tail, the lion's mane, and the bulk of the bull elephant seal—fashion statements advertising reproductive fitness. As we shall see, that's why there is a natural connection during the phallic stage between a developing awareness of the genitals and a developing sense of status. Being phallic-minded has its origin in Freud's description of a "phallic" stage of development, between the ages of about three and five or six years. During the phallic stage, we become curious about differences between the sexes and interested, in particular, in our own genitals. Boys become increasingly aware that they have a penis while girls become increasingly aware that they have a vagina and a clitoris.

Male and female experiences
The different experiences that boys and girls have of themselves anatomically during the phallic stage are reflected in the different Freudian symbols used to represent the sexes. Phallic symbols—

symbols that stand for the male's penis essentially and the social power associated with it—invariably portray male vigor and potency and are frequently potentially penetrative. Phallic symbols include swords, sabers, fountains, revolvers, umbrellas, ballistic missiles, powerful cars, and reptiles such as snakes. Female symbols represent the vagina and are generally receptive and passive. They include hollow containers such as coin purses, vases, and bottles, as well as ships, caves, valleys, and the interiors of buildings. A male Freudian friend of mine once claimed that men feel threatened by the demolition of tall industrial chimneys because, when they come crashing down, it symbolizes castration to them. To which a non-Freudian female friend replied that if that were the case women should feel correspondingly threatened by mining pit closures.

Phallic pathology

In addition to incubating Oedipal conflicts—those conflicts that have their origin in our relationship with our parents and which may later influence how we relate to the opposite sex—the phallic stage is also the birthplace of pathological sexual exhibitionism and voyeurism. Other phallic behaviors include power dressing, wearing flashy ties (symbolic penises), spitting (prevalent in young males, as it is said to symbolize ejaculation), and a dependence on status symbols. Phallic behavior is seen, too, in people who like to exert sexual power over others—by dressing provocatively, for example—and in those for whom single-minded ambition, self-centeredness, and the exploitation of others is a reason for living. These are phallic ways of behaving not least because the wielding of power ends up becoming, like masturbation, an end in itself.

Fact or fallacy?

Freud's assumption, typical at the time of the Austro-Hungarian Empire, of the preeminence of the phallus was to set him on a collision course with women. The crash was a particularly bad one because of his assertion that, merely because they do not have a penis, women go through life feeling inadequate, suffering from so-called "penis envy." What's more, if women do want to achieve, he argued, their ambition is simply an attempt to compensate for not having a penis. The trouble with this argument is that it's irrefutable: whatever a woman chooses to do, the theory is supported. Moreover, most women would argue that their exclusion from positions of power has had more to do with social history and male attitudes toward women than with differences between the male and female genitals.

In contrast to the individual who seeks power and status, the next questionnaire is about being a conformist. This can be traced, in Freudian terms, to a time in childhood when we were eager to please and to follow the rules of society.

How conformist are you?

Are you an independent thinker or do you follow the crowd? To what extent have you developed your own ideas?

		Yes	No
1.	Do you think it's important to be like other people?	☐	☐
2.	Would you say that you hold very different views from your parents?	☐	☐
3.	Do you think it's ever justified to be rude?	☐	☐
4.	Are you adventurous when it comes to trying new foods?	☐	☐
5.	Do you often worry about making a fool of yourself in public?	☐	☐
6.	If necessary, would you be prepared to break the law to retrieve something that had been stolen from you?	☐	☐
7.	Do you think children should always respect their parents?	☐	☐
8.	Do you think people who are eccentric are likely to have lower moral standards than people who are more conventional?	☐	☐
9.	Do you think children are exposed to too many negative role models on TV?	☐	☐
10.	Are you in most situations the person who makes the first move?	☐	☐
11.	Is having an interesting job more important to you than having a secure job?	☐	☐
12.	Do you think that rules were made to be broken?	☐	☐
13.	Do you enjoy the same music as your friends?	☐	☐
14.	Do you worry when filling in a form that if your answers are not absolutely truthful you may get into trouble?	☐	☐

15. Does it bother you to be in the minority? ☐ ☐
16. Do you think it's important to stick to society's rules no matter how trivial they may seem? ☐ ☐
17. If you met someone who turned out to have a criminal record, would you try not to see them again? ☐ ☐
18. Would you be offended if someone called you a sexual puritan? ☐ ☐
19. "Keep off the grass." Would you ever not? ☐ ☐
20. Would you like to be a model citizen? ☐ ☐

Interpret your score

Give yourself one point for each answer that matches the key:

1. Yes	5. Yes	9. Yes	13. Yes	17. Yes
2. No	6. No	10. No	14. Yes	18. No
3. No	7. Yes	11. No	15. Yes	19. No
4. No	8. Yes	12. No	16. Yes	20. Yes

0–4 You are an independent thinker, not a conformist. Conformists are important because they help to create stability in society and without stability we couldn't plan for anything. But the great thing about independent thinkers is that they bring about change in the world. If it weren't for people like you everything would stay the same.

5–10 You are both a rebel and a conformist—a Che Guevara and a neoconservative—happy to agree with the majority when their view corresponds with yours but equally prepared to be in the minority. In other words, you're pragmatic—when it suits you to do so you go with the flow, but you'll side with the rebels if it suits you better.

11–16 Crick and Watson, Franklin and Wilkins, Louis Pasteur, Rosa Parks, Albert Einstein—people who thought independently and by so doing changed the way that we view the structure of DNA, disease, race, and physics. You too are capable of being a non-conformer, but to do so you'll need to ignore the child in you that was taught always to do as you were told.

17–20 You are a dyed-in-the-wool conformist. Either through a process of osmosis or because you were brainwashed, you've almost completely adopted the views of those who brought you up. As a result, you don't have as many ideas of your own as you could have. If everyone thought like this nothing would ever change.

An interlude called latency

It was reported in a recent study that infant male vervet monkeys showed a preference for an orange ball and a police car, categorized as "boys' toys," while the infant females showed a preference for a human baby doll and a red cooking pot, categorized as "girls' toys." This dubious study doesn't prove that Freud was right when he claimed that anatomy is destiny (any more than does another study that used human infants) though, as we shall see, young school-age children do often try hard to conform. Being a conformist can be linked to his description of a period of "latency," between the ages of about five or six years and puberty. During this time, children direct their energies toward acquiring new skills and knowledge, both in school and in their play. Although sexual curiosity is not extinguished during this period, parents do not generally encourage sexuality.

Cultural influences
During latency, we are immersed in the culture of our parents and that of the society in which we live. In most cases, latency

children will have identified with the parent of their own sex at the end of the previous phallic stage. As a result of this identification, boys tend to imitate the skills of their fathers during latency, while girls tend to learn from their mothers. During this period of their development, boys typically play with boys, and girls typically play with girls. If we don't progress psychologically beyond this stage we could, in theory, be conformist as adults or feel awkward with the opposite sex through inexperience.

Whether you're a conformist or an independent thinker, there is one final stage of development. According to Freud, emotional maturity—what the next questionnaire is about—is only achieved when we reach the genital stage.

How emotionally mature are you?

Are you capable of caring for someone else apart from yourself?
Does give and take play a part in your relationships?

		Yes	No
1.	Have you found it difficult to form a lasting relationship?	☐	☐
2.	Are you, or would you like to be, in a stable and loving relationship?	☐	☐
3.	Does having an exclusive relationship with one other person make you feel claustrophobic?	☐	☐
4.	Do you have any unusual sexual preferences?	☐	☐
5.	Do you always try to consider your partner's feelings?	☐	☐
6.	Are you tolerant of other people's weaknesses?	☐	☐
7.	Does being intimate with another person embarrass you?	☐	☐
8.	Do you feel envious when other people do well?	☐	☐
9.	Do you enjoy pleasing your partner sexually?	☐	☐
10.	An open relationship is one in which both partners allow each other to have additional lovers. Appeal?	☐	☐
11.	Would you like to make more sexual conquests?	☐	☐
12.	Do you think sex is the most important thing in a relationship?	☐	☐
13.	If your partner were to lose their looks tomorrow, would you still love them for the person they are?	☐	☐
14.	Your partner loses their job. They turn to you for emotional support. Do you think you'll be able to give it?	☐	☐
15.	If your partner had to go into a psychiatric hospital, would you think any the less of them?	☐	☐

16. Do you think it's all right to cheat on your partner if you don't get caught? ☐ ☐
17. Is having a close confiding relationship with one other person high on your list of priorities? ☐ ☐
18. Do you think that loyalty is something to be valued in a relationship? ☐ ☐
19. Are you rather a selfish lover? ☐ ☐
20. Do you, or would you, enjoy being celibate? ☐ ☐

Interpret your score

Give yourself one point for each answer that matches the key:

1. No	5. Yes	9. Yes	13. Yes	17. Yes
2. Yes	6. Yes	10. No	14. Yes	18. Yes
3. No	7. No	11. No	15. No	19. No
4. No	8. No	12. No	16. No	20. No

0–4 You are emotionally immature. Instead of seeing a relationship as a two-way process, you seem to regard a partner as someone who's there to satisfy your needs and to whom you don't have to give anything in return. The idea of relating to a partner for the person they are rather than for what you can get out of them almost seems to have passed you by completely.

5–9 Having grit in any mechanism prevents it from functioning properly, and being emotionally selfish does the same for relationships. You know in theory, for example, that relationships involve give and take, but you don't seem to put this into practice on a regular basis. Until you start to consider the feelings of other people more consistently, your relationships will stay the way they are.

10–15 It's not easy to put an exact figure on emotions: in some ways you're more emotionally mature than other people and in other ways you're not. If you are in a relationship, you probably care for your partner most of the time and forget to do so at other times. You have the capacity to care for and to nurture someone else but are occasionally a bit amnesic about doing it.

16–20 If you are in a relationship, you are probably an excellent partner—partly because you're unselfish and partly because you try to understand how the other person feels; in other words, you are usually emotionally mature. Try not to lose sight of your own emotional needs though, or, by being excessively unselfish, make other people feel guilty.

On reaching the genital stage

When Freud died in 1939, the term "teenager" had yet to be coined to the sound of rock 'n' roll in the 1950s, and Elvis Presley was only four years old. But if they had met, Freud and Elvis would probably have got on well together, as they were both in the business of breaking down inhibitions. According to Freud, it is during the teenage years that the "genital" stage of development is reached, and with it emotional and sexual maturity. Ignited by the hormonal changes of puberty, the sexual instinct catches light again, but this time it is directed outside the family.

Freud's genital ideal
During the genital stage, the majority of young men and women become psychologically capable of forming a heterosexual relationship, expressed sexually in genital intercourse. To reach this stage presupposes that the preceding psychosexual stages, including the Oedipal phase, have been successfully negotiated. Although full adult sexuality is not achieved until the genital stage, residues of the earlier psychosexual stages persist into

adulthood and can be seen in, for example, kissing and foreplay. It follows that to be neurotically inhibited about sex, to have an interest in the genitals of your own sex, or to have any sexual fetish is to fall short of the genital ideal, as in theory an earlier stage has not been fully left behind.

Genital analysis

Freud's portrayal of the supremacy of the genital stage has been criticized by those women who see genital intercourse as a form of male domination and female humiliation. For them, genital intercourse is in no way a desirable goal, as it perpetuates women's subjugation by men. For different reasons—being attracted to your own sex could be genetic, for example—those who are homosexual have questioned Freud's interpretation of the origin of their sexual preference. Nevertheless, and despite the fact that Freud regarded heterosexuality as "normal" and anything else as "abnormal," the psychological aspects of the genital stage apply equally to long-term non-heterosexual relationships. This is because, in contrast to the sexual self-interest of the earlier phallic stage, the genital stage embodies, above all, the ability to form an unselfish, caring sexual relationship with another person.

This section has been about the different personality types associated with each of the psychosexual stages—oral, anal, phallic, genital, and latency period. Freud's contention was that if a person becomes fixated at any stage they will spend their life unconsciously trying to return to it. In today's terms, they may choose to become a celebrity chef, a banker, or a TV executive, depending at which stage they were fixated. However, although the personality types that Freud described so vividly undoubtedly exist, that doesn't mean that they necessarily originate in the way that he thought they do, even if most people would agree that the experiences of childhood influence us as adults.

It is during the phallic stage that boys are said to negotiate the Oedipus complex and girls the Electra complex (Freud used "Oedipus" when referring to both the sexes) and it is to these triangular relationships that we now turn. But before doing so, it seems important to mention that the next two questionnaires are based on Freud's assumption that the goal of psychosexual development is the ability to form a relationship with someone of the opposite sex. This means that there will be questions that you won't easily be able to answer if you don't happen to be heterosexual. There will be plenty for you to relate to though, as numerous aspects of our relations with our parents apply to heterosexuals and non-heterosexuals alike.

4 Freudian family life

If you want to know how Freud interpreted both male and female experiences of family life, you will need to answer both questionnaires in this section. As well as answering the question-naire that relates to your own sex, therefore, if you're a man, try to answer the Electra complex one by imagining how a woman might answer it and, if you're a woman, try to answer the Oedipus complex one by imagining how a man might answer it.

Do you have an Oedipus complex?

As a man, how much are you still influenced by the relationship that you had as a child with your parents? Are you still being influenced without knowing it?

		Yes	No
1.	Some people judge themselves by how well they do at work. Do you feel impelled to be successful in your work?	☐	☐
2.	Do you think that people in positions of power have a right to be looked up to?		
3.	Are you comfortable when other people are the center of attention?	☐	☐
4.	Do you think that people who don't make a success of their lives have only themselves to blame?	☐	☐
5.	Are you sometimes jealous of other people's relationships?	☐	☐
6.	Do you have a tendency to put women on a pedestal?	☐	☐
7.	When you were a child, did you identify with your father?	☐	☐
8.	Do some men make you feel inadequate?	☐	☐
9.	Have you ever secretly tried on an article of women's clothing?	☐	☐
10.	Do you ever worry about being castrated?	☐	☐
11.	Do you actually enjoy sexual intimacy with women?	☐	☐
12.	Are you sure that you are one hundred percent heterosexual?	☐	☐
13.	Do you sometimes like to denigrate women?	☐	☐
14.	Would you, or do you, feel comfortable having a woman as your boss?	☐	☐

15. Do you feel protective toward people who are weaker than you are? ☐ ☐
16. Have you ever accidentally referred to your girlfriend or partner as your mother? ☐ ☐
17. Do your thoughts about women ever make you feel guilty? ☐ ☐
18. Do you think that couples who kiss passionately in public should have it pointed out to them that their behavior may be offensive to other people? ☐ ☐
19. Are you extremely possessive when you're in a relationship? ☐ ☐
20. Do you enjoy the company of men and women equally? ☐ ☐

Interpret your score

Give yourself one point for each answer that matches the key:

1. Yes	5. Yes	9. Yes	13. Yes	17. Yes
2. Yes	6. Yes	10. Yes	14. No	18. Yes
3. No	7. No	11. No	15. No	19. Yes
4. Yes	8. Yes	12. No	16. Yes	20. No

0–5 If Freud hadn't thought of the Oedipus complex, it's unlikely that you would have done so. As far as you're concerned, size isn't a major issue and you don't spend much of your time worrying about being castrated. You have good relationships with men and women and are not afraid of intimacy. All in all, you appear to have successfully negotiated the Oedipal phase of your childhood.

6–11 Size matters—or at least it does to someone with an Oedipus complex—and when playing soccer they take extra special care to shield their genitals in the event of a free kick. This doesn't mean that you wouldn't take precautions in this situation, but your relationships with both the sexes are generally easygoing. Your development was not significantly arrested during the Oedipal phase of your childhood.

12–16 Size is an issue and you are competitive, but you are no longer so concerned about how high up the wall you can urinate. Your relationships with men and women are generally relaxed, except that sometimes, quite unexpectedly, you overreact to somebody as if you were still a child. This will continue to happen until you resolve more Oedipal issues from your childhood.

17–20 The saying "Two's company, three's a crowd" has a special meaning for you as, for much of the time, you are stuck in an Oedipal time warp. Sometimes you even feel jealous when you see someone reading a newspaper or talking on their cell phone, as you unconsciously feel that they're not paying enough attention to you. To exorcise such Oedipal ghosts, try relating some of these experiences to your childhood.

The influence of the Oedipus complex on men

The expectation at the end of a fairy story that the hero and the princess will live happily ever after reflects a child's hope that their own mother and father will always be together. Maybe this is why, even in an age of lone-parent families, the story of King Oedipus still has such universal appeal. Freud borrowed the name for the most famous of his complexes from classical Greek drama. In Sophocles' play *Oedipus Rex*, the Prince of Thebes unknowingly kills his father and marries his mother. When he discovers what he has done, he blinds himself as a punishment.

Origin of the Oedipus complex

In his description of the Oedipus complex, Freud contended that, if you are a man, between the ages of about three and six you would have liked to keep your mother exclusively to yourself. What stood between you and this incestuous ambition was the powerful figure of your father who, in fantasy, was ready to extinguish your desire by castrating you. Anxiety about this awesome punishment, coupled with your continuing desire to keep your mother to yourself, led to a jealous rivalry of your father's relationship with your mother. At the same time, wanting your father out of the way (literally dead) made you feel guilty. This then is the Oedipus complex: you desired your mother but were fearful of your father. To resolve the conflict you renounced your claim on your mother and became like your father. The reason you don't remember any of this is that the feelings were repressed and never put into words.

Effects of the Oedipus complex

Freud thought that a man's sexual interests are shaped by his Oedipal experiences. Hence, a man may look for a woman who is like his mother or for a woman with qualities that he would have liked her to have had. Other men seek relationships with women whom they feel they can safely despise—prostitutes, for example—so denying their love for their mother, whose image they keep pure and intact. This ambivalent male attitude toward women has been called the Madonna-whore complex and is conspicuous in Mediterranean cultures, though it occurs in other cultures too. When a man chooses another man as a partner he has, in Oedipal terms, assumed the identity of his mother instead of his father, so from a Freudian perspective (not a genetic one, though) his Oedipal development is incomplete. Another interpretation of why some men are not attracted to women involves the abstruse notion of a *vagina dentata* (vagina with teeth): unconsciously they fear that if they were to have sex with a woman they would lose their penis—a fear reinforced by the idea that a woman once had a penis but was castrated at some point, the evidence there to see in menstrual blood. In contrast, Freudian theory (ignoring biology) would argue that a male transsexual feels relief after surgery because he can then fuse psychologically with the mother he has identified with.

Oedipus in the workplace

The so-called "authoritarian personality type" has been described in Oedipal terms. Authoritarians are (usually) men who unquestioningly obey orders from their superiors while bullying their subordinates. The Freudian argument is that because they have not resolved their Oedipus complex, authoritarians are still unconsciously frightened of being castrated by their fathers, and this is why they continue to obey authority figures. To do this, they have to repress their own aggressive feelings, and it is these same feelings that they displace onto people weaker than themselves. In theory, Paul Kline reckoned, revolutionaries and men who clash with authority are also driven by an Oedipal desire to overthrow their fathers, while workaholics have an Oedipal need to prove themselves to their fathers.

Oedipal analysis

While not wanting to underestimate the importance of a mother to a young boy, Freud's account of the Oedipus complex may have been a projection of his own experience of having a young, attractive mother who doted on him and a much older father. It's not clear either, even allowing for a boy's discovery of his genitals and male/male rivalry, why castration should be the preferred punishment, except that biologically this would prevent reproduction with the mother. And, although a man's choice of partner may in part be influenced by memories of his mother, there are many reasons—social, economic, political, and religious to name a few—why a person may pursue a particular course in life.

Freud was less confident of his ability to understand women: "The great question that has never been answered, and which I have not yet been able to answer, despite my thirty years of research into the feminine soul, is 'What does a woman want?'" This didn't stop him from speculating about the psychology of women, and the next questionnaire is about the effect on a girl's adult life of her relationship with her mother and father.

Do you have an Electra complex?

As a woman, how far are your relationships still influenced by how you got on with your parents as a child? To what extent are you still being influenced unconsciously?

		Yes	No
1.	Do you think that women have an almost unplayable hand and that men have nearly all the cards stacked in their favor?	☐	☐
2.	Do you think that women make better lovers than men?	☐	☐
3.	Does power dressing appeal to you?	☐	☐
4.	Do you enjoy looking feminine?	☐	☐
5.	If the opportunity arises, do you think that women should use their sexuality to advance their careers?	☐	☐
6.	Do you ever feel envious of men?	☐	☐
7.	Did you enjoy playing with dolls as a child?	☐	☐
8.	If you had had a choice in the matter, would you have liked to have been born a male?	☐	☐
9.	Do you like to be noticed by men?	☐	☐
10.	As a little girl, did you enjoy being "made of sugar and spice"?	☐	☐
11.	Do you like men to treat you as one of the boys?	☐	☐
12.	Are you attracted to older men?	☐	☐
13.	Would you like to be able to urinate standing up like a man?	☐	☐
14.	Do you enjoy doing "girlie" things sometimes?	☐	☐
15.	Are you attracted to powerful men?	☐	☐
16.	Have you ever had, or would you like to have, sex with another woman?	☐	☐
17.	Do you think that women evolved to be more nurturing than men?	☐	☐

18. Generally speaking, do you enjoy the company of men? ☐ ☐
19. Have you ever looked for a father figure in a man? ☐ ☐
20. Are you usually quite contemptuous of men? ☐ ☐

Interpret your score

Give yourself one point for each answer that matches the key:

1. Yes	5. Yes	9. No	13. Yes	17. No
2. Yes	6. Yes	10. No	14. No	18. No
3. Yes	7. No	11. Yes	15. Yes	19. Yes
4. No	8. Yes	12. Yes	16. Yes	20. Yes

0–5 There's an interesting debate about whether a person who hasn't had a particular experience can fully comprehend the experience of a person who has. In this case, the fact that you are so far away from having an unresolved Electra complex may leave you wondering what all this talk of penis envy and father figures that we're getting into is all about.

6–11 "Penis envy . . ." — "Penis what?" All right, this may not be a major issue as far as you're concerned. You're quite happy, thank you, with the way you are and don't see men as having something down there that you would like as well. Nevertheless, and despite the fact you don't appear to have an unresolved Electra complex, the occasional turbulence you experience in your relationships could have something to do with unconscious childhood memories.

12–16 As far as having an Electra complex is concerned, you are inconsistent: at times you are womanly and sophisticated, at other times you're not. When taken in conjunction with the ups and downs of your relationships with men and women, this inconsistency suggests that you negotiated some childhood issues more successfully than others.

17–20 When Wordsworth wrote "The Child is Father of the Man," he probably didn't have being a feminist, a mistress, or a lesbian in mind—unlike Freud, who was always thinking about such things. In your case, consistent with having a partially unresolved Electra complex, the way in which you relate to men and women is sometimes a bit like it was when you were a child.

The influence of the Electra complex on women

Daddy's Little Princess is a term of endearment that reflects the natural affection of a father for his daughter. It's easy to forget therefore that when Freud described an Oedipal phase during a child's development he was writing not about the parents' feelings toward the child but about the child's feelings toward the parents. It was Freud's colleague Carl Jung who named the conflicts that arise during the Oedipal phase of a young girl's development the Electra complex. He chose this name because in Greek mythology Electra plots to have her mother killed in revenge for the murder of her father.

Origin of the Electra complex

In his account of a girl's Oedipal development—"Oedipal" used in a general sense in relation to both the sexes—Freud proposed that if you are a woman the person that you loved first was your mother, the same as it is for a man. Things started to go differently when, between the ages of about three and six, you became aware for the first time that, unlike boys, you do not have a penis—that, instead, you have a vagina and a clitoris.

Freud believed (and he has been criticized for saying so ever since) that this realization was like discovering that you had been castrated and why later, as a woman, you suffered from penis envy. In your unconscious mind, you blamed your mother for having allowed this thing to happen to you and for your being as powerless (without a penis) as you were. You wanted unconsciously to take your mother's place with your father because to give your father a baby would have compensated you, by association, for not having your own penis, especially if it had been a baby boy.

This then is the Oedipal riddle for girls: you felt drawn to your father but were frightened of losing your mother. To resolve the dilemma, you gave up the unconscious idea of a romance with your father and became like your mother. In part you did this to retain your mother's love and partly because the idea of being a mother became more appealing to you. As with the Oedipus complex, the feelings surrounding this phase were repressed and never put into words—hence, the influence on your adult life is an unconscious one.

Effects of the Electra complex

The way in which a girl negotiates the Oedipal relationship with her parents was said by Freud to influence her later sexual interests. In most cases, a girl's early love for her father is reawakened in adolescence and transferred onto men outside the family. However, some teenage girls, it is claimed, may become "accidentally" pregnant if they still have an unconscious need to compete with their mothers. Or, to get the attention of an undemonstrative father, a girl may unconsciously choose a boyfriend of whom she knows her father will disapprove. When a woman chooses another woman as a partner (genetics aside) she has not, in Oedipal terms, identified with her mother; hence she cannot accept the role a man can play in fulfilling her sexual needs. A woman who is still in love with her father may find relationships with other men inadequate. Or she may derive satisfaction from being a mistress, as this allows her to separate other couples who remind her, unconsciously, of her own parents.

In theory, it follows that female high achievers and worka-holics are unconsciously driven by penis envy (unlike those who give up on ambition when they discover they don't have a penis) and that women who prefer older men unconsciously see them as father figures. Likewise, a woman who learns as a little girl that a successful way of getting her father's attention is to be flirta-tious without serious intent may carry this forward as an uncon-scious strategy with other men in later life.

Electra analyzed

Why a biologically normal girl would feel that she has been castrated, would be envious of boys, or would want to share her father's penis in order to make a baby has never been satisfac-torily explained by Freudians. The American neo-Freudian Karen Horney perversely suggested that men suffer from "womb envy" and indeed, leaving social influences to one side for a moment, it could in part be because they cannot become pregnant that men are able to be such natural-born achievers. Despite Freud's apparent devaluation of women though, psychoanalysts such as Juliet Mitchell have argued that Freud did help to explain the unconscious mechanisms by which boys and girls acquire an unequal sense of their worth. According to the psychoanalytic theorist Nancy Chodorow, this psychological inequality is perpetuated by non-shared parenting: because of their sexual difference from their sons (a difference reinforced by the taboo on incest), mothers unconsciously propel their sons into the world to become independent, while fostering dependence in their daughters. Followers of the French psychoanalyst Jacques Lacan argue that such inequalities are unconsciously acquired when children learn language, as language traditionally reflects the dominant (male) culture. In what might be seen as an attempt to castrate Freud himself, the philosopher and linguist Luce

Irigaray described women as the self-touching sex for whom, vaginal lips forever rubbing and embracing, men are redundant.

Our unconscious memories of our parents are some of many that Freud thought that we carry forward from the past: Oedipal memories might lead us to choose a partner who is like a mother (to look after us) or a father (to protect us), for example. The next section focuses on the mechanism by which this happens, but before that it travels back to a time when we were too young to know who our mother was, and later considers whether there is a darker side to our character of which we are usually unaware.

5 Birth, life, and death

The questionnaires in this section are about how much you love yourself, to what extent you live out the past in the present, and whether you have a self-destructive streak. They are based on Freud's writings about narcissism and transference, and his speculations about a "death instinct."

How narcissistic are you?

Are you preoccupied with yourself or are you interested in other people? Do you feel that you're an outsider or a fully paid-up member of society?

		Yes	No
1.	Do you prefer your own company to that of other people?	☐	☐
2.	Does the fantasy of having an audience of millions appeal to you?	☐	☐
3.	Are you sometimes rather cold and aloof?	☐	☐
4.	If there's a mirror in a room, do you tend to look in it?	☐	☐
5.	Do you sometimes feel unreal?	☐	☐
6.	Do you spend a long time getting ready to go out?	☐	☐
7.	Would you describe yourself as warm and friendly?	☐	☐
8.	Do you feel rather superior to other people?	☐	☐
9.	Are you more practical than imaginative?	☐	☐
10.	Are you sometimes a bit of an emotional loner?	☐	☐
11.	Do you find it easy to make friends?	☐	☐
12.	Do you sometimes feel that you're a fake?	☐	☐
13.	Are most people, in your opinion, rather second rate?	☐	☐
14.	Do you sometimes feel like an alien from another planet when you're with other people?	☐	☐
15.	Do the people you're with sometimes seem like aliens from another planet?	☐	☐
16.	Does anyone really know you?	☐	☐
17.	Do you mix easily with other people?	☐	☐
18.	Do you find it easy to trust other people?	☐	☐
19.	Do you live life as an onlooker?	☐	☐
20.	Do you allow people to get close to you emotionally?	☐	☐

Interpret your score

Give yourself one point for each answer that matches the key:

1. Yes	5. Yes	9. No	13. Yes	17. No
2. Yes	6. Yes	10. Yes	14. Yes	18. No
3. Yes	7. No	11. No	15. Yes	19. Yes
4. Yes	8. Yes	12. Yes	16. No	20. No

0–5 You will understand better than most people what John Donne meant when he wrote "No man is an island, entire of itself," as you are hardly narcissistic at all. On the contrary, you're interested in other people and enjoy the company of friends. All right, you're capable of being a bit withdrawn and preoccupied, but for the most part you feel yourself to be a fully paid-up member of society.

6–11 You swing between being interested in other people and being self-absorbed. To your friends you're like a temperamental air-conditioning system — warm and sociable some of the time, at other times cold and aloof. Your friends value your company and accept your need to withdraw from time to time. Narcissistic? Occasionally.

12–16 Appearances are deceptive as far as you and being narcissistic is concerned. You can be a bit remote and unapproachable, but you are also interested in other people and can be sociable when you want to be. Despite the fact that you do enough to get by, there are times when you feel alienated from society. No one would guess that you sometimes feel insecure and vulnerable.

17–20 Cue the opening music of the film *2001 — A Space Odyssey*. You are a bit like an astronaut circling high above Earth in your own orbit, encased against a hostile environment. You can be quite narcissistic and mistrusting of other people. Although you give the appearance of being self-assured, you are sometimes vulnerable and mask your insecurity behind a show of strength.

Narcissism and self-esteem

"Mirror, mirror on the wall, Who is the fairest one of all?" asks Snow White's stepmother. A case for Sigmund Freud perhaps. Certainly, readers of celebrity magazines will recognize the narcissism and the self-obsession. The word "narcissism" comes from the mythological Greek figure, Narcissus, who caught sight of himself in a pool of water and fell in love with his own reflection. In everyday speech, to be narcissistic means to be preoccupied or in love with yourself, and sometimes has the connotation of a sexual perversion.

Primary narcissism
In "On Narcissism: An Introduction" (1914) Freud uses the term narcissism to refer to our initial relationship to our own body when we are first born. He thought that during this earliest narcissistic stage of development we have an intense and, for the most part, solitary relationship with our own body, deriving pleasure and stimulation from ourselves. Only when we have developed some primitive sense of our self (our ego, in other words) can we transfer our interest toward the outside world and form what is a second relationship with our mother or caregiver.

Secondary narcissism
The identification of a primitive, narcissistic stage of development has had implications for how psychoanalysts think about and treat psychological problems. Freud interpreted our neurotic preoccupations (anxieties, phobias, obsessions, and so forth) in terms of things that go wrong after the narcissistic stage in our relations with our parents. But, and in the absence of modern

scientific knowledge, he thought that the so-called psychotic disorders (such as the schizophrenias) involve regression to the earlier narcissistic stage of development. When it came to treatment, he had noticed that narcissistic patients found it difficult to make use of psychoanalysis if they were still narcissistically attached to themselves rather than interested in other people. Although there have been therapeutic developments since Freud, in a classical analysis a part of your ego needs to be able to form a therapeutic alliance with the analyst so that you can work with the analyst and understand interpretations.

Narcissism and relationships

In contrast to the influence of the Oedipal phase, which might make us choose a partner who is like a mother or a father, "narcissistic object choice" is when we choose a partner who reflects a real or imaginary part of us. We may, for example, choose a partner who has qualities that we already possess; alternatively, we may look for qualities that we would like to possess (femininity, masculinity, beauty, or ambition, for example). The danger of this is that if, through death or the breakdown of a relationship, for example, we lose someone close to us who contains a part of us in this way we may feel empty (and, hence, depressed) because they take a part of us away with them when they go. Despite these drawbacks, psychoanalysts regard "healthy narcissism" as an integral part of our makeup, because if we did not love ourselves at all we would suffer from very low self-esteem.

The next questionnaire is about how much emotional baggage you're carrying from childhood and reflects the recurrent Freudian theme that our early childhood experiences influence how we later perceive the world.

How much are you influenced by the past?

Do you live in the present or are you still in the past? How much emotional baggage are you carrying from your childhood?

		Yes	No
1.	Do you sometimes wonder what's become of people you've lost touch with?	☐	☐
2.	Can you remember what it felt like to be at your first school?	☐	☐
3.	When you have a meal, do you feel it's important to finish everything on your plate?	☐	☐
4.	Is it important to you to have the latest gadget?	☐	☐
5.	Can you remember the color of your first bicycle?	☐	☐
6.	Do you remember who you first had a crush on?	☐	☐
7.	Is being fashionable important to you?	☐	☐
8.	Can you name five or more people you were at school with?	☐	☐
9.	Can you remember the names of three of your teachers?	☐	☐
10.	Do you think that change is usually for the better?	☐	☐
11.	Rather than wait, do you throw things out before they're worn out?	☐	☐
12.	Do any of the seasons remind you of your childhood?	☐	☐
13.	Do you still feel the influence of your parents— for example, when you make decisions?	☐	☐
14.	Do you like to return to places that you knew as a child?	☐	☐
15.	Have your values changed much over the years?	☐	☐
16.	Do you like contemporary art as much as the work of Old Masters?	☐	☐
17.	Are there certain foods (ones you had at school, for example) that still remind you of childhood?	☐	☐

18. Do you switch channels when a program on archeology or an ancient civilization comes on? ☐ ☐
19. Do you think that your schooldays are the best days of your life? ☐ ☐
20. Would you like to live in a newly built house or apartment in preference to an old one? ☐ ☐

Interpret your score

Give yourself one point for each answer that matches the key:

1. Yes	5. Yes	9. Yes	13. Yes	17. Yes
2. Yes	6. Yes	10. No	14. Yes	18. No
3. Yes	7. No	11. No	15. No	19. Yes
4. No	8. Yes	12. Yes	16. No	20. No

17–20 "Stands the Church clock at ten to three? / And is there honey still for tea?" In the same way that time is frozen in poet Rupert Brooke's lines about the old vicarage at Grantchester, so you too are living in a bit of a time capsule. It sometimes seems as though the world has moved on while you've stood still. As long as you view the world through a veil of the past you won't see things as they really are.

11–16 Taxidermy is the art of stuffing dead animals to be put on display. Sound familiar? All right, this is an exaggeration, but you do sometimes have a tendency to be nostalgic and to live in the past, though this doesn't take you over completely. Nevertheless, and despite the fact that you're not always open to change, you generally see the world as it is.

5–10 Like lazy brown trout on a hot summer's afternoon, memories of your childhood swim just below the surface, occasionally causing ripples and influencing your work and your relationships. Generally, though, rather than dwell on the past you try to get on with your life, and for the most part you do so successfully.

0–4 If history teaches us anything, it teaches us that people don't learn from it: on a global scale, people continue to fight wars; on a personal level, they continue to repeat the same mistakes. Only when you can fully acknowledge the influence of the past will you be able to make sense of the present. At the moment you're not doing this as much as you could.

Transference: the influence of the past

The experience of time is relative: to the young it goes on forever, to the old there's not enough of it; when we're interested in something it flashes by, when we're bored it crawls along interminably. It's relative in another way when we travel back to the past in memory and when we project ourselves into the future to make plans. When forgotten childhood memories influence what we do as adults, this is the kind of time travel that Freud called "transference."

The transference relationship

When a person is in psychoanalysis, transference has a special meaning to do with how they relate to their analyst. By revealing few, if any, personal details Freud remained a mystery to his patients and this encouraged them to transfer or project their childhood experiences and fantasies onto the resulting analytic "blank screen." When a person admires, values, or even loves their analyst these feelings are called positive transference. Negative transference is when a person is contemptuous and disparaging of their analyst. In both cases, Freud believed these unnaturally strong feelings to be replays of feelings that the person felt previously toward their parents or toward other significant people in their childhood, such as teachers and brothers and sisters. Psychoanalysis, he thought, gives a person the opportunity to examine these feelings and to test them against reality.

Countertransference

Freud tried to relate to his patients as the dispassionate scientist he'd been trained to be—if a patient made him experience an emotion, he would try to disregard it. This approach changed markedly within psychoanalysis following the publication in 1950 of a paper entitled "On Countertransference" by Paula Heimann. Today, psychoanalysts are more likely to interpret what a person makes them feel—the countertransference—as a form of communication. If, for example, a person makes their analyst feel more intelligent than they know they really are—or, for that matter, completely useless—the analyst may interpret their own reaction to being made to feel this way in an attempt to understand the person better. Does the person, in the first case, for example, lack confidence in their own ability? Do they, in the second case, have an unconscious need to disparage their analyst to make themselves feel better? It is important for an analyst not to confuse their own feelings with what the person makes them feel (this can range from sexual attraction to boredom). In theory, having undergone their own analysis makes this less likely.

In *Further Learning from the Patient* (1990), the psychoanalyst Patrick Casement describes working with a patient who had begun to talk so quietly in her sessions that he was hardly able to hear what she was saying, which he began to sense might be an important communication. Rather than ask her, again, to speak louder, he told her that he thought there was something important about the way in which she was talking to him, that it made him realize that he would need to listen very carefully to her—as a mother might to her infant before it can talk—and that he sensed she was feeling that he didn't understand her. The patient began to cry. What had made the difference, she explained, was the fact that he understood that he didn't under-stand—unlike her parents who had often assumed that they understood her when they didn't.

Analyzing transference

The ability to understand and to interpret what's going on in the transference relationship is a key part of how psychoanalysis works. Firstly, this is because the feelings the patient transfers onto their analyst reveal distortions about the way in which they view their analyst. Secondly, analysis of these distortions reveals similar unconscious distortions in the patient's relationships with other people. In everyday life what gets carried forward from childhood to adulthood often gets transformed: what was experi-enced in relation to a parent may now be experienced in relation to a lover; what was experienced in a school situation may now be experienced at work. Psychotherapy takes place when a person is able to separate what they have imported from the past from the reality of what's happening in the present.

The last questionnaire in this section is based on Freud's belief that, in addition to being creative, we also have a natural tendency to be self-destructive.

Do you have a death wish?

Do you have a positive or a negative outlook on life? How often do you sabotage things when they're going well?

		Yes	No
1.	Do you usually think about the consequences of your actions before you do something?	☐	☐
2.	Do you tend to repeat the same mistakes?	☐	☐
3.	Are you often your own worst enemy?	☐	☐
4.	"Always look on the bright side." Do you, usually?	☐	☐
5.	Have you ever had unprotected sex with someone you didn't know very well?	☐	☐
6.	Are you usually able to express your feelings?	☐	☐
7.	Is feeling low a rare event in your life?	☐	☐
8.	Have you ever purposely injured yourself?	☐	☐
9.	Do you think about death at least once a month?	☐	☐
10.	Do you think about death every week?	☐	☐
11.	Do you think about death every day?	☐	☐
12.	Do you think about death on your birthday?	☐	☐
13.	Have you ever imagined your own funeral?	☐	☐
14.	Are you careful to avoid taking risks?	☐	☐
15.	Do your relationships with the opposite sex (same sex if appropriate) tend to be love-hate relationships?	☐	☐
16.	Gloomy thoughts are the exception in your life, not the rule?	☐	☐
17.	Is your behavior ever reckless to the point of being dangerous or life threatening?	☐	☐
18.	Have you ever thought about killing yourself?	☐	☐
19.	Do you often wonder what it would be like not to exist?	☐	☐
20.	Have you ever been a Buddhist?	☐	☐

Interpret your score

Give yourself one point for each answer that matches the key:

1. No	5. Yes	9. Yes	13. Yes	17. Yes
2. Yes	6. No	10. Yes	14. No	18. Yes
3. Yes	7. No	11. Yes	15. Yes	19. Yes
4. No	8. Yes	12. Yes	16. No	20. Yes

0–5 Death wish? Not generally for you. Although capable of gloomy thoughts, you believe in the power of positive thinking and try to look on the bright side of life. You find it hard to understand people who get depressed, let alone people who commit suicide. Self-reproach and self-hatred are not words that figure much in your vocabulary—being negative about things isn't usually your style.

6–11 It's about as rare for you to have a death wish as it is for the French to overcook their food. So when things are going well it's incomprehensible to you that anyone should not find life worth living. In your darker moments you sometimes wonder what the point of life is, but on balance you are driven by a zest for life, not by melancholic musings.

12–16 "'Forward, the Light Brigade! / Charge for the guns!' he said: / Into the valley of Death / Rode the six hundred," wrote the poet Alfred Lord Tennyson. And the chances are you wouldn't have been amongst them. Why? Because, although you sometimes have a death wish, when you ask yourself what the point of life is you can usually come up with a reasonable answer, and you generally have sufficient insight not to give in to seriously self-destructive urges.

17–20 Although you don't deliberately step in the path of fast-moving vehicles, some of your behaviors can be unconsciously self-destructive at times. It is not unknown for you to take unnecessary risks, for example, or, occasionally, to sabotage your own success. You would be less self-destructive if you were you to become more aware of your unconscious and let people know how you feel.

Freud's death instinct

In an Indian parable about karma a young man hears that Death is about to come for him. To avoid Death he travels to the next village. Death is surprised to see him there because, following a change of plan, he was no longer going to be visiting the young man's village. The message of the story is that you cannot escape your destiny. However, Freud argued that for unconscious reasons people may well play a part in their own downfall (for example, when they drink to excess or smoke) and so invite death to visit them prematurely. The notion of a "death instinct," or "death drive," and thereby a death wish, is one of Freud's more controversial ideas, a theory of self-destruction that he formulated in the wake of the carnage of World War I.

Toward oblivion

In his paper "Beyond the Pleasure Principle" (1920) Freud contended that the goal of the death instinct is to return us to a state of non-existence, our closest memory of which is the blissful state of Nirvana that we originally experienced in the womb or at the breast. Since it is imperative to avoid being annihilated by this self-directed death wish, Freud came to believe that we redirect the death instinct away from us in the form of destructiveness toward other people. It appears in an eroticized form in sadomasochistic practices and is unsuccessfully deflected in suicide.

Freud drew his evidence for the death instinct from several different sources. He had noticed how traumatized soldiers from the battlefront relived their horrific experiences in their dreams and in their everyday thinking. He was struck how children repeat in their play, as well as in their dreams, what they don't understand or what frightens them (giving injections, playing teacher, being the dentist). And he saw how often we repeat the same mistakes (choosing a partner who is bad for us more than once, for example) without apparently learning from them. Freud interpreted this compulsion to repeat as an attempt on our part to make sense of the world in order to reduce our overall level of tension. Through a convoluted piece of Freudian logic, reducing tension then became synonymous with seeking a state of peace or oblivion; hence he famously wrote: "The aim of all life is death."

Love and hate

The destructive force of the death instinct, corresponding to Thanatos, the personification of death in Greek mythology, is opposed in Freud's theory by the creative force of the "life instinct," or Eros, the god of love in Ancient Greece. In the perpetual struggle between love and hate, the death instinct not only gains the upper hand in the case of suicide but is present, too, in cases of self-inflicted injuries and depression, and in cases of alcoholism and drug addiction. Following Freud's example, addiction to gambling was interpreted by the psychoanalyst Edmund Bergler in the 1950s as a form of masochism—an example of "turning against the self." In some instances, the death instinct is expressed both outwardly and inwardly. In World War II, Japanese kamikaze pilots deliberately flew their planes into US targets, inflicting as much damage as possible on the enemy and in the process killing themselves. Islamic suicide bombers and hijackers have likewise blown themselves up with those they regard as the enemies of Allah, in the belief that they are guaranteeing themselves a place in paradise.

Freud had earlier thought (biology aside) that depression involves a regression to the oral stage of development. The concept of a death instinct provided him with another way of looking at it: because civilization imposes tight controls on the expression of the death instinct, he thought that we re-incorporate part of its destructiveness into our superego. The result of not expressing our "bad" feelings is that instead we punish ourselves by means of our conscience with self-reproach and self-hatred, and this, he argued, leads to depression. He had anticipated this in his paper "Mourning and Melancholia" (1917), in which he argued that self-reproach arises in the case of mourning from not being able to express what we feel toward the person who has died, and in the case of depression from not expressing our hostile feelings in general. Although the concept of the death instinct has itself provoked considerable love and hate among psychoanalysts since Freud, the notion of a "death wish" is in everyday use.

Freud was forever applying psychoanalytic principles to new areas of life. The questionnaires in the next section concern three areas that were dear to his heart: the interpretation of dreams, Freudian slips, and jokes.

6 Dreams, slips, and jokes

Freud wrote about dreams, Freudian slips, and jokes in quick
succession (1900, 1901, and 1905) and linked all three to the
unconscious.

Are your dreams trying to tell you something?

Freud claimed: "The interpretation of dreams is the royal road to a knowledge of the unconscious activities of the mind." What state of repair is your dream life in?

		Yes	No
1.	Are you ever frightened of going to sleep because of what you think you may dream about?	☐	☐
2.	Do you sometimes have very vivid dreams?	☐	☐
3.	Have you ever been woken up by a nightmare?	☐	☐
4.	Do you have a particular dream that recurs?	☐	☐
5.	Do you think that people try to read too much into dreams?	☐	☐
6.	Have you ever confused something that you've dreamed about with real life?	☐	☐
7.	Do you remember, on average, less than one dream per week?	☐	☐
8.	Would it be a waste of time for you to keep a dream diary?	☐	☐
9.	Have you ever had a series of dreams in which each was related to the other?	☐	☐
10.	Can you remember any dreams that you had as a child?	☐	☐
11.	Do you stop listening if someone starts to recount a dream that they've had?	☐	☐
12.	Would you sometimes like to dream the same dream again?	☐	☐
13.	Can you remember having a nightmare when you were a child?	☐	☐
14.	Have you ever woken up remembering a dream and in the evening still been trying to interpret it?	☐	☐
15.	Do you have trouble remembering your dreams?	☐	☐

16. Is trying to interpret your dreams a pointless exercise as far as you are concerned? □ □

17. Can you claim never to have had a sexually explicit dream? □ □

18. Have you ever solved a problem in a dream? □ □

19. Do you sometimes do unusual things in your dreams? □ □

20. Some scientists think that dreams should be regarded solely as electrochemical activity. Do you think they're right? □ □

Interpret your score

Give yourself one point for each answer that matches the key:

1. Yes	5. No	9. Yes	13. Yes	17. No
2. Yes	6. Yes	10. Yes	14. Yes	18. Yes
3. Yes	7. No	11. No	15. No	19. Yes
4. Yes	8. No	12. Yes	16. No	20. No

17–20 Sometimes your dreams are so vivid that they make you feel as though you're on drugs. To achieve equivalent experiences, Aldous Huxley took mescaline, Carlos Castaneda took peyote, and in California in the 1960s the Flower Children took LSD. You're not exactly clear what your dreams mean but they sure feel like they mean something.

11–16 Going to sleep is always an adventure, as you never know where you're going to end up or what's going to happen. Sometimes the images in your dreams are reminiscent of the works of Surrealist artists and moviemakers—Salvador Dalí, René Magritte, Luis Buñuel, Federico Fellini. Even though at other times they're less strange, it's hard to imagine that your dreams don't mean something.

5–10 A recording of your brain's activity when you're asleep would reveal that, like everyone else, you experience rapid-eye-movement dream sleep for fifteen minutes, four to five times every night. However, maybe because you don't want to delve too deeply into your unconscious, you don't always remember your dreams. Let your mind wander freely and you will remember more of them.

0–4 No one knows what newborn babies dream about but research has shown that they spend more of their time in dream sleep than adults do. The relevance to you is that just as there is no evidence that newborns remember their dreams so, when you wake up in the morning, it sometimes feels as if the past eight hours haven't existed. To become more aware of your dreams, encourage your ego to drop its guard more often.

The interpretation of dreams

Lights! Camera! Action! When we're asleep each of us becomes an Oscar-winning movie director: great screenplays, unlimited budgets, stunning cinematography—the drama compels us to think that our dreams mean something. It's not surprising therefore that Freud wrote in 1931 that he thought his book *The Interpretation of Dreams* contained "the most valuable of all the discoveries it has been my good fortune to make"—and that your dreams would have been of special interest to him. When we are asleep, he argued, our unconscious mind has the opportunity to bypass the internal censorship of what he was later to call the superego. If we then free associate to what has come to the surface—to what we have dreamed about, in other words—our conscious mind has a unique opportunity to work through a layer of unconscious thoughts and feelings.

Dreams as wish-fulfilments

According to Freud, dreams are not merely random brain activity but, triggered by "day residues," the active creations of our unconscious mind. Just as neurotic symptoms contain strangulated versions of feelings we cannot fully express, so dreams are disguised versions of what we would like to be happening—in other words, they are wish-fulfilments.

What we experience as a dream Freud called the "manifest content" of the dream, though even this is subject to "secondary elaboration" when we wake up and try to remember it. What lies behind the dream he called the "latent content," which is the dream's meaning. He described dreams as the "guardians" of our sleep, believing that the disguise of the manifest content allows us to remain asleep.

The dream-work process

The latent content of a dream is transformed into its manifest content by "dream-work." Dream-work is woven by the anarchic, unregulated thought processes of the id. This is why our dreams may appear irrational or "insane" when viewed by our ego in the light of day. However, while our dreams may be closer to "insanity" than we may wish to think, they are also a normal way of expressing what we are feeling unconsciously.

The most common dream-work mechanism is "dramatization." This is the way that we experience our wishes and desires in dreams in visual, movie-like images. This medium lends itself to "condensation," which is when unrelated elements in a dream are fused together, and to "displacement," which is when we disguise something significant by relocating it in another scenario.

The most talked about mechanism in dreams is "symbolism." Some symbols are said to have universal meanings—kings and queens representing parent figures, for example—but, of course, symbols have very personal meanings, too. For example, walking through the streets of a deserted city in a dream might symbolize a feeling of inner emptiness to one person, but to someone else it could symbolize longed-for solitude. Freud's associate Sándor Ferenczi reported a patient's dream in which she strangled a small white dog. Free association suggested that the dream expressed an unconscious desire to kill her sister, who was known to have a pale complexion—and a few days earlier she had called her "a biting dog." An American psychoanalyst's interpretation of a girl's dream about a man trying to mount a very frisky small brown horse was that the dreamer was attracted to the man in question, her own pet name from childhood being *cheval*, French for "horse." Two other mechanisms that help to disguise the latent meaning of a dream are when we trivialize what is important to us and when we change things into their opposites.

Other kinds of dreams

Freud acknowledged that there is a problem in interpreting all dreams as disguised wish-fulfilments. After all, it is common to have dreams that cause us anxiety, dreams in which traumas are relived, and undisguised sexual dreams. On the other hand, Freud's way of looking at dreams opened up a new vista into the mind and, through the method of making free associations to dreams, a way of exploring them, as well as being an influence on twentieth-century painting, literature, and moviemaking.

In the same way that our ego can be caught off guard when we're asleep, so Freud thought that our everyday mistakes reflect what we're thinking about unconsciously. The next questionnaire investigates the extent to which any lapses of concentration that you have or accidental slips that you make may be self-motivated.

How accident-prone are you?

If you slip on a banana skin, is it your fault or is it someone else's fault? Are any of your slipups of the Freudian variety?

		Yes	No
1.	Have you ever sent a text to the wrong person?	☐	☐
2.	In the heat of the moment, do you sometimes say things you don't mean to say?	☐	☐
3.	Do you keep a first-aid box in your home in case of emergencies?	☐	☐
4.	Have you ever been told something in confidence and then accidentally told someone else?	☐	☐
5.	If you have an important decision to make, do you prefer to sleep on it?	☐	☐
6.	If you're on a diet, do you easily forget about it?	☐	☐
7.	If you're meeting with friends, are you usually the first to get there and then have to wait for them to arrive?	☐	☐
8.	Have you ever forgotten to set your alarm clock?	☐	☐
9.	Have you ever forgotten to turn the bath water off?	☐	☐
10.	Are you good at remembering important birthdays and anniversaries?	☐	☐
11.	Have you ever let a pan boil dry?	☐	☐
12.	Do you know where to turn off the water supply in your home in the event of an emergency?	☐	☐
13.	Have you ever accidentally overshot your station or bus stop?	☐	☐
14.	Have you ever locked yourself out?	☐	☐
15.	Can you claim never to have been accidentally overdrawn at the bank?	☐	☐
16.	Have you ever inadvertently left a shop without paying for something?	☐	☐

17. Have you ever deleted a file from your computer only to find that you later needed it? ☐ ☐
18. Do you plan and book your vacations well in advance? ☐ ☐
19. Do you ever accept invitations from people and later wish that you hadn't? ☐ ☐
20. Have you ever completely forgotten to do something you said you would do? ☐ ☐

Interpret your score

Give yourself one point for each answer that matches the key:

1. Yes	5. No	9. Yes	13. Yes	17. Yes
2. Yes	6. Yes	10. No	14. Yes	18. No
3. No	7. No	11. Yes	15. No	19. Yes
4. Yes	8. Yes	12. No	16. Yes	20. Yes

0–4 If you have any kind of insurance policy, you probably have a protected no claims bonus, as you don't appear to be very accident-prone. Most things you do are meticulously planned, nothing much being left to chance. Remember to listen to your unconscious, too, though, because otherwise you could be in for some nasty surprises.

5–10 Some accidents, such as being struck by lightning, are outside of our control, but we can all be caught unawares by things that we haven't thought about. Although you generally look before you leap, accidents of the second type still occasionally happen to you—but then no one can ever fully predict what their unconscious is going to do.

11–16 You are no more accident-prone than other people and no less aware of the influence of your unconscious. By your own admission, though, you are apt to forget things and to put your foot in it from time to time. Clumsy? Not really. You have the occasional accident and don't always see things coming— nothing unusual about that.

17–20 If you have life insurance, consider increasing it. Frankly, you have more accidents than you need to, though bearing in mind that you don't always reflect on why you do things, this is hardly surprising. If you were to pay more attention to your unconscious, you would find that events you regard as random are more self-motivated than you think they are.

Freudian slips

If a person accidentally drives down a one-way street in the wrong direction and someone gets killed, they get into more trouble than if no one is killed. The legal logic behind this would have been of interest to Freud as, in between writing about dreams and jokes, he wrote in *The Psychopathology of Everyday Life* (1901) about some of the everyday mistakes we make. However, he would probably have been even more interested to know what it was that unconsciously made the person lose their concentration in the first place. What has become known as a "Freudian slip," or "parapraxis" (*fehlleistung* in the original German), is when you appear to do something accidentally but, really, you have an unconscious motive for doing it. Accident-prone or not, we are all capable of upsetting a drink or misspelling a word, forgetting an appointment or a name. Freud believed that these "accidents" and lapses of memory are not actually accidental at all but are caused by our unconscious.

Hidden motives
Freud's explanation of why we make mistakes and have lapses of concentration is based on the principle of psychic determinism,

which is that all mental events are caused by previous experiences stored in the unconscious. Seen like this, Freudian slips are close relatives of dreams, jokes, and neurotic symptoms, as each in its own way provides an outlet for the unconscious. According to Freud, when we do something accidentally, our ego has dropped its guard, just as it does in a dream, and it is this that allows an unconscious impulse to take over.

Freud's interpretations of his own and other people's accidental slips are frequently long and ingenious, running into several pages. A concise example involved a patient who nearly invited his estranged wife to join him in England from the USA aboard a ship that he "accidentally" forgot had been torpedoed and sunk some years earlier. In another example, provided to Freud by Jung, a man could not remember a line in a poem about a snow-laden pine tree covered "with the white sheet." When asked by Jung to free associate to these words, the man thought of the linen sheet a corpse was wrapped in, of his brother who had recently died of a heart condition, and of his own fear of dying from heart disease. Jung's interpretation of this lapse of memory was that the man could not recall the line because it had an unconscious association with his repressed fear of death.

There are many everyday examples of Freudian slips: we leave things in places we want to return to; we "forget" appointments we don't want to keep; we phone the wrong person "by mistake." Every day, according to Freud, we stumble, spill, avoid, and slip—all the time concealing motives of which we remain unaware.

Minding the gap
By using the unconscious to interpret both accidental slips and neurotic symptoms (in addition to dreams and jokes) Freud reduced the distance between what is regarded as "normal" and what is regarded as "abnormal." Sometimes our defenses slip and what is just submerged comes to the surface (swearing is an

example). Sometimes we accidentally displace one thought into another—like the patient mentioned earlier who initially wrote *Lusitania* instead of *Mauretania* when inviting his wife to join him in England. And sometimes, in order to avoid what we cannot remember, we forget completely.

The next questionnaire is based on Freud's belief that your unconscious is revealed not only in your dreams and in the mistakes you make, but also in the jokes that make you laugh.

Do you have a Freudian sense of humor?

Freud regarded jokes as an outlet for the unconscious. Do you use humor to make yourself feel better?

	Yes	No
1. Do you ever make, or laugh at, jokes about any of the following: age, sex, religion, death, bodily functions?	☐	☐
2. Do you remember ever laughing uncontrollably as a child?	☐	☐
3. Do you think that some topics should be off-limits as far as making jokes is concerned?	☐	☐
4. Do you sometimes laugh at other people's misfortunes?	☐	☐
5. Do you generally switch to something different when there is a comedy show on TV?	☐	☐
6. Do you sometimes make jokes about things that really you're frightened of?	☐	☐
7. Do you feel embarrassed wearing a party hat?	☐	☐
8. Do you sometimes use humor to try to break the ice with people you don't know very well?	☐	☐
9. Is sex an emotionally neutral topic as far as you're concerned?	☐	☐
10. Have you ever felt like laughing during a horror movie?	☐	☐
11. Do you like playing practical jokes on people?	☐	☐
12. Do you feel inhibited laughing out loud in front of other people?	☐	☐
13. Do you sometimes laugh nervously when you're anxious?	☐	☐
14. If you were advertising for a partner on a dating site, could you seriously claim to have a good sense of humor?	☐	☐

15. Do you find it difficult to make jokes at your own expense? ☐ ☐

16. Do you remember exchanging dirty jokes with other children when you were a child? ☐ ☐

17. Have you ever been unable to stop laughing when you wanted to? ☐ ☐

18. Do you think that it's time some people took life more seriously and stopped making fun of everything? ☐ ☐

19. Do you sometimes make jokes to avoid being serious? ☐ ☐

20. Does it bother you if other people make jokes at your expense? ☐ ☐

Interpret your score

Give yourself one point for each answer that matches the key:

1. Yes	5. No	9. No	13. Yes	17. Yes
2. Yes	6. Yes	10. Yes	14. Yes	18. No
3. No	7. No	11. Yes	15. No	19. Yes
4. Yes	8. Yes	12. No	16. Yes	20. No

16–20 If having a good sense of humor is the aphrodisiac that people say that it is, just think what such a high score could do for your love life. Your sense of humor provides an important outlet for your unconscious that helps you, with few exceptions, to keep things in perspective and to see the funny side of life. Useful when things go wrong.

10–15 They say that what goes up must come down. That's especially true of yo-yos, and in their case recovery is almost instantaneous. In the same way, your sense of humor usually helps you to keep things in perspective and, although you sometimes take yourself too seriously and fail to see the funny side of things, this doesn't last long and before you know it you're back up again.

5–9 Charlie Chaplin, W.C. Fields, Laurel and Hardy, and the Marx Brothers. They all helped Freud and his contemporaries not to take life too seriously. You, too, are capable of poking fun at the self-important and are not immune from laughing at other people's misfortunes. This provides a useful escape valve for your unconscious, but you could afford to open it more often.

0–4 There are moments when you seem to suffer from a sense of humor failure. When this happens, you take yourself and life extremely seriously and forget to recall the saying "Laugh and the world laughs with you, cry and you cry alone." At risk of sounding like a textbook, humor is important because it provides an indirect route to your unconscious, so allowing you to express what would otherwise remain bottled up.

Jokes and the unconscious

If Freud were alive today he would almost certainly have enjoyed stand-up comedy and sit-coms on TV, as his analysis of what it is that makes us laugh didn't stop him from having a good sense of humor. Far from it. When he first sent some of his dream inter-pretations to Wilhelm Fliess, his friend and confidant, Fliess wrote back saying that some of them sounded more like jokes than anything else. Rather than take offense at this, Freud started to take jokes seriously, to collect them and to write about them, publishing *Jokes and Their Relation to the Unconscious* in 1905.

Getting past the censor
Freud included jokes in the same category as dreams, neurotic symptoms, and Freudian slips—jokes, according to Freud, reveal

a good deal about the workings of our unconscious mind. Looked at like this, jokes allow us to express subversively what we usually try to keep unconscious—not surprisingly, jokes are often cruel or sexual. When you find a joke hilariously funny, what's actually happening, according to Freud, is that you're momentarily bypassing the censorship of your superego and expressing what you really feel. Jokes can only reach your unconscious in this way because they follow an indirect route— a joke is no longer funny if it is too explicit or undisguised, as it can no longer get past your unconscious defenses.

Freud's theory of jokes fits into his economic model of the mind, in which libido circulates around the mental system under varying pressures. If you explode with laughter when you hear a particular joke, for instance, Freud believed this to be because there has been a sudden release of energy, the force of the explosion being in direct proportion to the amount of energy you've been using to keep the idea behind the joke repressed.

The form and content of jokes

Freud thought that a part of the pleasure of all jokes is the way in which they are told. Just as we are influenced by the style of a work of art, so Freud saw the words used to tell a joke as a sort of "forepleasure" to the main content of the joke.

We often find jokes funny because they allow us to lift our own personal inhibitions—jokes about sex, for example—or because they undermine social repression—for example, political satire. Frequently, the two work together: we project what we are personally frightened of happening to us onto other people. So, if a person finds great relief in jokes about homosexuality and mental disability, they may be sexually insecure and unsure of their own mental abilities. It is clear through our laughter (or our deliberate suppression of it) that we don't find the topic of sex as neutral as, say, that of doing the dishes.

Joking aside

When a person is with their analyst, the jokes they make can give some insight into how their unconscious works and into what is on their mind. But making jokes can sometimes be a form of resistance, too—for example, if they deflect attention away from something else, like changing the subject or arriving late for a session, each in its own way also being a communication from the patient.

Dreams, Freudian slips, and jokes all involve our ego being unguarded, which then allows our unconscious to express itself. The next section, and the two that follow it, are based on the defense mechanisms that Freud and his daughter, Anna Freud, thought that we use to prevent this from happening.

7 Freudian defense mechanisms that deny reality

Freudian defense mechanisms can be divided into categories: those that deny reality, those that distort reality, and those that falsify it. Although there is overlap between the categories, the questionnaires in this section are mostly about denying reality.

How repressed are you?

Are you a truly liberated individual or are you rather inhibited? How far do you conceal your feelings even from yourself?

	Yes	No
1. During the past two months have you seriously indulged yourself?	☐	☐
2. Can you usually let yourself go at weekends?	☐	☐
3. Do you find it hard to recall events from childhood?		
4. Are there certain matters that are so personal you won't even discuss them with your friends?	☐	☐
5. Are you ever the life and soul of the party?	☐	☐
6. Are you very conventional sexually?	☐	☐
7. If some friends invited you to do karaoke with them to raise money for charity, would you?	☐	☐
8. Do you sometimes blurt out things and then regret that you said them?	☐	☐
9. Do you worry about exposing more of your body during the summer months?	☐	☐
10. Do you tend to say what you feel even if it offends other people?	☐	☐
11. If you won the equivalent of three months' salary, would you choose to spend it rather than save it?	☐	☐
12. Do you believe in the adage "Out of sight, out of mind"?	☐	☐
13. Do you ever like to do things on the spur of the moment?	☐	☐
14. Would you like to have a go on a trampoline?	☐	☐
15. Are you a devoutly religious person?	☐	☐
16. Do you think that talking about death is morbid?	☐	☐
17. Do you think that the censorship of movies and games should be increased?	☐	☐

18. If your partner suggested something new to spice up your sex life, do you think you'd be interested? ☐ ☐
19. Do you sometimes prohibit yourself things unnecessarily? ☐ ☐
20. Do you think that there should be more rules in society? ☐ ☐

Interpret your score

Give yourself one point for each answer that matches the key:

1. No	5. No	9. Yes	13. No	17. Yes
2. No	6. Yes	10. No	14. No	18. No
3. Yes	7. No	11. No	15. Yes	19. Yes
4. Yes	8. No	12. Yes	16. Yes	20. Yes

17–20 You are inclined to live under a repressive regime of your own making, your thoughts and feelings protected by concrete blocks, CCTV, and razor wire. You sometimes worry that if these defenses were not in place you would be in some kind of danger. This tendency to censor what you say and what you think means that even some of your friends don't know much about you.

11–16 During prohibition in the United States, people used to drink illegally, which tells us something about human nature—when you ban things, you don't get rid of them, they just go underground. In your case, you don't always find it easy to express your feelings, but neither are you a hostage to your unconscious.

5–10 You are like one of those novelty barometers: one character comes out to signify rain, the other to signify sun. That's why people who know you divide into two camps: those who regard you as inhibited and easily embarrassed and those who see you as quite self-indulgent. The truth is probably somewhere between the two.

0–4 *Liberté, égalité, fraternité, ou la mort!*—you are, for the most part, a truly liberated individual, wrapped in a revolutionary flag, whose thoughts and feelings come tumbling out without any trouble at all. As far as your emotions are concerned, you stand shoulder to shoulder with your fellow citizens in the crowd at the Bastille. You are hardly repressed at all.

Repression—Freud's theory of forgetting

The danger of repression can be seen in the number of Roman Catholic priests who, denied access to a natural sex life, sexually abused children. "Repression" is the most fundamental defense mechanism that we possess and refers in psychoanalysis to the unconscious process by which we try to banish from our mind thoughts and feelings that are causing us anxiety. Unlike suppression, which we do consciously, repression (also known as "motivated forgetting") is an unconscious process, so we are unaware of doing it. One of the most interesting things about Freud's theory of forgetting is the idea that we forget things not because they are unimportant to us but because they are so significant.

From reality to fantasy
Freud's original theory of what gets repressed is known as the "childhood seduction theory." Based on what his patients told him and the relief, or catharsis, that they felt after telling him, Freud thought that his patients' emotional distress was the result of repressing their memories of being sexually abused as children.

Between 1900 and 1910, Freud changed his theory to one involving fantasy—the controversial theory of infantile sexuality and fantasy. Rather than actual childhood seduction, he came to believe that what his patients were reporting were "screen memories" or fantasies of what they had imagined or feared could have happened. He believed that these fantasies were most likely to have arisen during the Oedipal phase of their development when children have very passionate feelings about their parents and when the affections of the opposite-sex parent may be sought. This tied in with his theory that children are sexually aware from an early age and that we pass through stages of psychosexual development.

Fact and fiction

Freud has been accused—for example, by his critic Jeffrey Masson—of changing his original theory merely because it was unpopular, though Freud himself reported that the change followed his own self-analysis and the emergence of an Oedipal theory, following the death of his father. Masson claims that it is because he changed his theory from one based on real events to one involving fantasy that victims of rape and sexual abuse have been routinely disbelieved. But Freud's two theories are not mutually exclusive: there are some patients who have been sexually abused and there are some patients who have not been sexually abused, but there is no patient who has grown up in a world devoid of human imagination. Psychoanalysis is concerned with both domains: the external world where things really happen and the inner world of the person where things are experienced.

Freud's economic model of the mind

Repression is part of Freud's economic model, which sees the mind as a "closed energy system" in which primitive instinctual energy, or libido, is constantly circulating, demanding release. It reflects nineteenth-century thinking about science and engineering, in particular the use of steam and hydraulics in mechanical systems. Repression is what makes the unconscious dynamic and gives it a life of its own, but it requires the expenditure of a great deal of energy. In economic terms, this is because the impulses that have been repressed are constantly striving to become conscious while we, at the same time, are unconsciously trying to keep the lid on them.

The next questionnaire is about being "in denial," a common expression today and a recurrent theme in Freudian theory.

Are you honest with yourself?

How often do you tell yourself the truth? How often do you lie to yourself?

		Yes	No
1.	Do you avoid having routine medical checks?	☐	☐
2.	When you are in a crowded place, are you alert to the possibility of a terrorist attack?	☐	☐
3.	Do you ignore the risks of flying?	☐	☐
4.	Do you ever worry about the threat of nuclear war?	☐	☐
5.	Do you sometimes make up fantasies about yourself?	☐	☐
6.	Have you ever gone on regardless when you knew there wasn't any point?	☐	☐
7.	Have your plans for the future turned out to be realistic so far?	☐	☐
8.	Do you sometimes try to put on a brave face?	☐	☐
9.	Are you planning for a secure financial future?	☐	☐
10.	Do you sometimes pretend that you don't care when really you do?	☐	☐
11.	Do you often turn a blind eye to things?	☐	☐
12.	To take a bull by the horns is risky, but so is turning your back on it. When it comes to dealing with problems, are you a matador?	☐	☐
13.	Do you think much about the effects of global warming?	☐	☐
14.	Have you ever said that you weren't frightened when really you were?	☐	☐
15.	Do you ever reflect on your friends' shortcomings?	☐	☐
16.	If you were threatened with redundancy, would you try not to think about it?	☐	☐

17. Do you take more than normal precautions against being mugged, raped, or otherwise attacked? ☐ ☐

18. Have you ever denied the evidence of your own eyes? ☐ ☐

19. Are you usually prepared to face your problems head on? ☐ ☐

20. Are you as fit as you think you are? ☐ ☐

Interpret your score

Give yourself one point for each answer that matches the key:

1. Yes	5. Yes	9. No	13. No	17. No
2. No	6. Yes	10. Yes	14. Yes	18. Yes
3. Yes	7. No	11. Yes	15. No	19. No
4. No	8. Yes	12. No	16. Yes	20. No

17–20 Under post-hypnotic suggestion a person can be made to believe something that plainly isn't true. In the same way, you have the capacity to blank things out and to ignore what you don't want to know. However, as you appear to have completed this questionnaire so honestly, you may be what is known in hypnosis as an "honest liar."

11–16 The difference between being economical with the truth and telling a lie is that, in the first case, you don't do something while in the second case you do do something. But in both cases the aim is to deceive, so that when you ignore your feelings from time to time or, occasionally, don't see things that are staring you in the face, it's you that you're not being honest with.

5–10 The author Quentin Crisp wrote in his memoir that if you don't do any housework the dirt doesn't get any worse after the first four years—his way of dealing with something that he didn't want to know about. Although you sometimes deceive yourself in order to boost your ego, you don't usually sweep things under the carpet completely. For the most part, you see things as they really are.

0–4 You are, for the most part, as honest as the day is long. Like an arctic explorer leaning into a blizzard, far from censoring what you feel, generally speaking you insist on facing the world head on. Not for you a world of make-believe and fantasy. Rather, you prefer to experience what life throws at you without flinching—assuming, that is, that you completed this question-naire honestly.

Denial as a defense mechanism

Holocaust denial is the claim that the genocide of Jews before and during World War II either did not happen or has been exaggerated. Given his experiences of the Nazis in Vienna, Freud would have been personally interested to understand this. (After his own death, four of his sisters in 1942 became victims of the Final Solution: Dolphi died of starvation in the Jewish ghetto at Theresienstadt, and Rosa, Mitzi, and Pauli were murdered in the concentration camp at Treblinka.) "Denial" in psychoanalysis describes the way that when we feel unable to say that we're sad or angry, for example, or to admit that we feel lonely or frightened, we may try to resolve the conflict (and so protect our ego) by pretending that it's not true. We're dishonest in this way in two respects: either we refuse to perceive something that really exists—ignoring a lump in the breast, for example—or we may say that we don't feel something when really we do—saying we don't care when we care a great deal, for example.

Denial in everyday life

As with all defenses, denial distances a person from their feelings. For instance, to protect their self-esteem, a person may deny obvious signs that their partner is having an affair. Or in order to deny what we feel about ourselves we may fantasize that we are more attractive or more potent than we really are, perhaps wearing high-fashion clothes or driving a powerful car to match the image. As children, we denied that we were tired when it was time to go to bed; as adults, we may deny the ageing process by dying our hair.

For and against denial

As a way of adjusting to events gradually, denial is a useful mechanism. We use denial when we grieve the death of someone close to us, refusing to believe that we will never see them again. A person may deny that they have a terminal illness even when the symptoms have been made clear to them. In some occupations, an element of denial is a prerequisite: soldiers, race drivers, and stuntmen need, at times, to deny the possibility of sudden injury and death. Nurses, doctors, and paramedics routinely deny some of their feelings to get through the day.

The trouble with persistent denial is that you end up not knowing what your real feelings are. During psychoanalysis, denial is often part of an overall resistance to being open and honest about your feelings. A patient who declares "there was never a cross word in our family" is probably denying the true atmosphere in their family, as well as concealing what they feel about their family. It is very common when in analysis, especially in the early stages, to deny being angry, sad, resentful, or despairing—even to acknowledge having any feelings at all.

The next questionnaire is about another way of denying reality— in this case by not acting our age, what Freudians call "regression."

How grown-up are you?

Do you always act like an adult or do you sometimes behave like a child?

		Yes	No
1.	Do most people seem to be more mature than you are?	☐	☐
2.	Do your friends regard you as someone they can rely on?	☐	☐
3.	Do you feel resentful if you can't get your own way?	☐	☐
4.	Does it sometimes feel as if there is nothing new in the world?	☐	☐
5.	If you get the chance, do you like to sleep for long periods of time?	☐	☐
6.	Do you usually think about the consequences of your behavior?	☐	☐
7.	Do you usually arrive on time for appointments?	☐	☐
8.	Do you still have, or do you wish that you had, some of your childhood toys?	☐	☐
9.	Are you easily swayed by other people's opinions?	☐	☐
10.	Are you responsible with money?	☐	☐
11.	Are you easily distracted away from a task that you have to do?	☐	☐
12.	In an ideal world, would you like to have everything done for you?	☐	☐
13.	Do you enjoy the challenge of responsibility?	☐	☐
14.	Are you someone people turn to for advice?	☐	☐
15.	Do you get very excited about new ideas?	☐	☐
16.	Do you enjoy being the center of attention?	☐	☐
17.	Do you enjoy being pampered?	☐	☐
18.	Do you sometimes cry when things go wrong?	☐	☐

19. Do you prefer savory foods such as olives, cheese, ☐ ☐
    and nuts to sweet foods such as cookies, cake, and
    ice cream?
20. Do you frequently change your mind? ☐ ☐

Interpret your score

Give yourself one point for each answer that matches the key:

1. Yes	5. Yes	9. Yes	13. No	17. Yes
2. No	6. No	10. No	14. No	18. Yes
3. Yes	7. No	11. Yes	15. Yes	19. No
4. No	8. Yes	12. Yes	16. Yes	20. Yes

0–4 "When I was a child, I spake as a child, I understood as a child, I thought as a child: but when I became a man, I put away childish things." These words could have been written especially for you, as you nearly always behave like an adult and take even small things seriously. Even when it would be natural for you to do so, you don't always find it very easy to behave like a child.

5–10 For most of the time you are like a sensible pair of shoes— loyal and dependable, come rain or shine, no matter what the terrain. That's why most people who know you regard you as a responsible and trustworthy adult. What they don't see is that sometimes, when you're under extreme pressure, for example, you're inclined to vacillate—more like a pair of flip-flops.

11–16 Adolescents are well known for wanting to do their own thing and to make their own decisions—and for expecting to find the fridge full of their favorite foods when they get in late at night. You're a bit like this: grown-up most of the time, but when the going gets tough you're capable of shifting responsibility onto other people.

17–20 When the writer J.M. Barrie created Neverland, he populated it with characters such as Peter Pan and Wendy, Tiger Lily, Tinker Bell, and Captain Hook. It seems that you too are quite often to be found in Neverland; unlike Peter, though, you only occasionally regress to being a child and are not intent on remaining one.

Regression — going back in time

You only have to see an adult engrossed in a Harry Potter novel, mesmerized by a display of toys in a department store, or riveted to the screen of a games console to know that being a child can be an attractive option. According to Freud, our adult life is built on the foundations of childhood and the more pressure we are under the more we are likely to use the defense mechanism of "regression," unconsciously becoming like a child to avoid facing what we feel we can't deal with.

Back to childhood

From time to time we all regress. Examples of regression include throwing tantrums, bursting into tears, and losing our temper. Thumb sucking and nail biting are seen by Freudians as regressions to the oral stage of development when, as babies, we tried things out by putting them in our mouth. By the same logic, taking to bed and adopting the fetal position is a regression to the womb.

Many people feel like children when they have to see their doctor or when they meet a head teacher. Being physically ill leads to regression and, in this case, we may need to be nursed like a baby. A special case of regression is argued to occur in the eating disorders of anorexia and bulimia. In the first case, extreme dieting keeps the body childlike, so that feelings associated with adulthood and adult sexuality are avoided; bingeing, in contrast, is a way of looking after yourself in a very oral way.

When a person lies on the analytic couch, a therapeutic form of regression is induced because by doing so they are partially relinquishing control of their ego. This makes it easier for them to access earlier phases of their life and to see how the "child" in them is intruding into their everyday life.

The next questionnaire looks at sublimation, a defense mechanism that blends so seamlessly into life that it is considered to be the only truly successful defense mechanism.

How well adjusted to society are you?

How far do you adapt your instincts to fit in with society? To what extent do you act out your instincts without restraint?

		Yes	No
1.	Do you enjoy dressing up to go out?	☐	☐
2.	Do you care what other people think of you?	☐	☐
3.	Do you think it's all right to break the law if you can get away with it?	☐	☐
4.	Have you ever raised money for a charity by asking people to sponsor you?	☐	☐
5.	Do you have a tendency not to think before you act?	☐	☐
6.	Do you enjoy breaking rules just for the sake of it?	☐	☐
7.	Have you ever committed a violent crime?	☐	☐
8.	Do you care about the effect your behavior has on other people?	☐	☐
9.	Is it more important not to get caught doing something immoral than it is not to do it?	☐	☐
10.	Some people think that the world owes them a living. Are you one of them?	☐	☐
11.	Do you think that graffiti is a socially acceptable form of artistic expression?	☐	☐
12.	Would you describe yourself as a neurotic kind of person?	☐	☐
13.	Do you usually try to dress to suit the occasion?	☐	☐
14.	If you were invited to a wedding and did not have the right outfit, would you be prepared to hire one?	☐	☐
15.	Do you ever throw litter in the street?	☐	☐
16.	Do you feel that society accepts you for the person you are?	☐	☐

17. Is your behavior sometimes raw and impulsive? ☐ ☐
18. If you were given a ticket to the circus, would you go? ☐ ☐
19. Do you enjoy going away on vacation? ☐ ☐
20. Would the size of your carbon footprint make you change your vacation plans? ☐ ☐

Interpret your score

Give yourself one point for each answer that matches the key:

1. Yes	5. No	9. No	13. Yes	17. No
2. Yes	6. No	10. No	14. Yes	18. Yes
3. No	7. No	11. No	15. No	19. Yes
4. Yes	8. Yes	12. No	16. Yes	20. Yes

0–4 When you choose to live your life without a thought for anyone else you are a social misfit. On those occasions, the idea of modifying your behavior to fit in with other people doesn't seem to enter your head. What you don't seem to realize—or at any rate not consistently—is that in their raw form your instincts don't appeal to other people.

5–9 According to social psychologists, social norms such as waiting in line, giving up your seat to a pregnant woman, and not playing your music too loudly on public transport are informal, agreed ways of behaving. When it comes to this kind of social adjustment, you're a mixture: in some situations you don't seem to comprehend the rules; in others the opposite is true.

10–15 "Do you have any bad habits?" is a type of question posed by psychologists in personality tests. Answer "Yes" and you're being truthful. Answer "No" and you're lying. In your case, although you don't always consider the effect of your behavior on other people, you would probably be classified as reasonably well adjusted to society whichever way you answered.

16–20 Our animal-evolutionary past refers to what we have inherited from our ancestors over millions of years and which, according to evolutionary psychologists, continues to influence us today. Given that you cannot escape your instinctual past completely, you are probably, with a few exceptions, as well adjusted to society as you can hope to be.

The cultural defense of sublimation

Try staging a gay pride march in Tehran, wearing a bikini in public in Saudi Arabia, or holding an atheists' convention in the Bible Belt of America. Different places, different rules. But, since our instincts haven't changed much over millions of years, Freud's ideas about expressing them remain as important as when he wrote about them. In psychoanalysis "sublimation" is when we rechannel primitive, socially unacceptable instincts into socially acceptable activities such as sport and culture. Freud regarded sublimation as a very useful defense mechanism, as these substitute activities allow us to express, in part, impulses that in their raw form would not be tolerated by society. Unlike neurosis (in which there is too much inhibition) and perversion (in which inhibition is lacking), sublimation allows us to adjust to society by redirecting our basic instincts along socially approved pathways.

What we sublimate

Many of the things we do can be interpreted as sublimations of more basic instincts. Those who take part in blood sports such as hunting are legally permitted to express their murderousness. In contact sports such as ice hockey, basketball, and soccer, and in martial arts and boxing, competition and aggression are ritualized. There are some prescribed sports, notably mountaineering and auto racing, where to take risks is acceptably suicidal. (An interesting combination of the murderous and the suicidal exists in bullfighting.)

How sublimation works

According to classical Freudian theory, sublimation permits the id's internal primary process world to have secondary process expression in the real world. To be an artist or to work in clay, for example, is interpreted by Freudians as an acceptable sublimation of the infantile urge to mess and to smear during the anal stage. Ballet dancing, it is claimed, is a sublimation of a child's instinctual enjoyment in displaying and being seen—a form of exhibitionism. This is mirrored in the voyeurism of the audience, derived from a child's instinctual pleasure in watching and looking at others (scopophilia). Most cultures regard uninhibited exhibitionism and voyeurism as "perversions."

Sublimation: for and against

Sublimations are a necessary part of life as it is socially unacceptable to express, among others, undisguised oral, anal, and Oedipal impulses. In preference to gluttony or alcoholism, oral impulses are better sublimated into being a restaurant critic or a wine connoisseur. The anal erotic instinct is frequently sublimated, too, into collecting, hoarding, and parsimony or into the reactive virtues of orderliness, cleanliness, and punctuality. Arguably, executioners satisfy their instinct to kill by doing it judicially, while gynecologists sublimate their interest in women into an occupation where they can legitimately examine them on medical grounds. However, while sublimation works for the individual, it may be bought at the expense of others. For example, when the superego is relieved of responsibility by the state, individual aggression, expressed in collective violence against a group, may be politically and socially sanctioned.

Examples have included pogroms in tsarist Russia and the Soviet Union, anti-Semitism in Nazi Germany, and the re-education of intellectuals during the Chinese Cultural Revolution.

Although contemporary psychoanalysts regard creativity and aesthetics in a more positive light, Freud thought that all cultural exploits—art and literature, music and science—are, in part, sublimations of more primitive impulses that allow dammed-up libidinal energy safe expression. This is why Freud saw sublimation not only as a necessary defense mechanism for the individual but also, under the right circumstances, as humanity's best hope for a non-neurotic future.

With Freud the obvious often turns out to be the unexpected, and so it is with the defense mechanisms in the next section. As with all defense mechanisms, each is designed to protect the ego, but each in the process distorts reality.

8 Freudian defense mechanisms that distort reality

The questionnaires in this section are about holding extreme views, making excuses, and distancing ourselves from our feelings. Each reflects Freud's belief that what you see is rarely what you get.

Are you an extremist?

Do you hold very strong views or are you easygoing and liberal? Is everything up for discussion or are some things non-negotiable?

		Yes	No
1.	Are there some people that you just can't stand?	☐	☐
2.	Do you get very hot under the collar over certain issues?	☐	☐
3.	Do you think a discussion should have a winner and a loser?	☐	☐
4.	If you can't get your point across, do you feel your blood pressure rising?	☐	☐
5.	Are you interested in other people's views?	☐	☐
6.	Do you find it easy to relax?	☐	☐
7.	Do you admire the powerful leaders in history?	☐	☐
8.	A friend of yours has a problem they want to talk about. Would you find it easy to listen?	☐	☐
9.	If you went to a multiplex and the movie you wanted to see was no longer showing, would you settle for a different one?	☐	☐
10.	Are you good at explaining things to people who don't understand straightaway?	☐	☐
11.	Are you really passionate about some causes?	☐	☐
12.	Do you get exasperated with people who don't see things the way you do?	☐	☐
13.	Do other people regard you as flexible?	☐	☐
14.	Do you obsess about things?	☐	☐
15.	Are you a relaxing person to be with?	☐	☐
16.	Do you talk more loudly if people don't agree with you?	☐	☐
17.	Tolerant. Your middle name?	☐	☐
18.	Are you known for your diplomatic skills?	☐	☐

19. Do you see compromise as a sign of weakness? ☐ ☐
20. In a discussion do you usually take the middle ☐ ☐
    ground?

Interpret your score

Give yourself one point for each answer that matches the key:

1. Yes	5. No	9. No	13. No	17. No
2. Yes	6. No	10. No	14. Yes	18. No
3. Yes	7. Yes	11. Yes	15. No	19. Yes
4. Yes	8. No	12. Yes	16. Yes	20. No

17–20 Postmodernists see the world in relative terms—not just one Shakespeare, for example, but many Shakespeares, a different version constructed by each reader. You, in contrast, are for the most part an unreformed extremist. On some issues there's no holding you back. It doesn't matter what other people say—if they don't agree with you, there must be something wrong with them.

11–16 You try not to be an extremist but you don't always succeed. You try to hold back and then suddenly bang! you let go—you've taken a stand on something you didn't even know you had a view on. Your extremism is not generally planned but, rather, a reaction to other people's views, so it rarely takes you over completely.

5–10 As far as being an extremist is concerned, you are inconsistent. Not that words such as "easygoing" or "lackadaisical" describe you any better. When you do take up the torch on behalf of a cause you can be quite a formidable opponent. For a while the flame burns brightly, but your enthusiasm doesn't always last and you sometimes end up back where you started.

0–4 Nothing wrong with being wafted around on the breezes of other people's opinions as long as you're just sampling them. To this extent you are the complete opposite of an extremist. You rarely hold any really strong views. You take life as it comes and can't understand why people get so frustrated when others don't agree with them. You would find it difficult to be a zealot—you don't believe in anything strongly enough.

Reaction-formation: going to the opposite extreme

Anyone caught in the flash of an extremist's bomb as they make their way to heaven may not immediately think of Freud, yet the motivation to hold such extreme views is something that Freud reflected on when he wrote about the defense mechanism of "reaction-formation." As with any defense mechanism, the aim of a reaction-formation is to keep the unconscious unconscious—in this case by obscuring what you really think or feel by saying or doing the opposite. Going to the opposite extreme creates a smokescreen behind which you conceal what you really feel. As with all defense mechanisms, the feelings you repress are primitive ones, the strength of the reaction-formation being in proportion to your need to repress them.

A "virtuous" defense mechanism

A reaction-formation can often be recognized precisely because it is so extreme. Sexual puritanism, for example, may be a cover for repressed sexual lust. The same applies to those who have given up addictions to pleasures such as alcohol, drugs, or gambling who become zealous campaigners against the "vices" that formerly held such a fatal attraction. Freud would not have been surprised by the results of a study that revealed homophobic males to be more likely than non-homophobic males to be sexually aroused by gay pornography.

Anal personality types who are obsessed with being clean and tidy exhibit a classic Freudian reaction-formation. These "virtuous" characteristics are seen by Freudians as a reaction-formation against a more infantile wish to mess and to play with their feces during toilet training—parental prohibitions against doing this having been adopted in an extreme form.

A close relative of the anal personality is the passive-aggressive type. Unable to express their feelings of rage on the outside, these people are habitually mild and deferential. This does not mean that all pacifists are repressed warmongers or that all vegetarians are repressed meat eaters, nor for that matter that psychotherapists don't care about their patients. However, a parent who is overindulgent and ineffective could be unconsciously paralyzing themselves in order to conceal an unconscious, perhaps murderous, resentment toward their child.

Disadvantages of reaction-formation

When they are extreme, reaction-formations can become neurotic symptoms—at least as seen in psychoanalytic terms—although some would disagree with this. Compulsively washing, for example, has been interpreted as a way of unconsciously trying to control violent feelings and so reduce feelings of guilt. In the same way, a compulsion to check whether light switches or the gas have been turned off can be seen as an unconscious attempt to control underlying violent impulses. At a primitive level, we might like the gas and electricity systems to blow up or catch fire—the opposite of what we think we believe. In other words, the inherent dangers of the gas and electricity reflect our own "lethal" feelings. This is why we are so ambivalent about leaving them on/turning them off.

In addition to their transparency to other people ("The lady doth protest too much, methinks," responds Gertrude in Shakespeare's *Hamlet*), reaction-formations have been said to have other disadvantages. First, it wastes a lot of energy to repress our feelings by expressing the opposite of what we feel.

Second, using reaction-formations implies that we do not know ourselves very well (since we are doing the opposite of what we really wish). Third, if we experience reaction-formations as real, as with any defense mechanism, we risk losing touch with what we really feel and, hence, with reality.

Having considered how much of an extremist you are, the next questionnaire looks at how good you are at making excuses.

How good are you at making excuses?

Are you good at explaining things away? Do you always have an excuse up your sleeve? Can you always find a way to justify what you do?

		Yes	No
1.	Do you frequently have second thoughts after you've made a decision?	☐	☐
2.	Many people go out of their way to prove themselves right. Do you ever try to prove yourself wrong?	☐	☐
3.	If things don't go according to plan, is your philosophy "It'll all come out in the wash"?	☐	☐
4.	Do you think that some things are just inevitable?	☐	☐
5.	Do you usually try to make the best of a bad job?	☐	☐
6.	When shopping, if you make a bad buy, does it bother you for the rest of the day?	☐	☐
7.	Rather than excuse other people their bad behavior, do you tend to confront them about it?	☐	☐
8.	Do you have a tendency to underestimate the environmental damage that you cause?	☐	☐
9.	Do you often feel the need to confess things?	☐	☐
10.	Do you generally overlook your own mistakes?	☐	☐
11.	If you have to be somewhere and you're running late, do you usually have an excuse ready before you get there?	☐	☐
12.	"Anything for an easy life." Could this be your motto?	☐	☐
13.	Do you find it very difficult to justify buying something that you can't really afford?	☐	☐
14.	Can you (if you don't play, could you) reconcile buying a lottery ticket each week with never winning anything?	☐	☐

15. Some people are exceptionally good at concealing the truth from themselves. Are you one of those people? □ □
16. Can you easily admit when you're wrong? □ □
17. Do you think that most things in life are for the best? □ □
18. Does it take you long to recover from a setback? □ □
19. Do you tend to ignore inconsistent evidence if it doesn't suit your argument? □ □
20. If you break the rules, do you always have a good reason for doing so? □ □

Interpret your score

Give yourself one point for each answer that matches the key:

1. No	5. Yes	9. No	13. No	17. Yes
2. No	6. No	10. Yes	14. Yes	18. No
3. Yes	7. No	11. Yes	15. Yes	19. Yes
4. Yes	8. Yes	12. Yes	16. No	20. Yes

16–20 The great escapologist Harry Houdini was able to free himself from a locked, water-filled, glass and steel cabinet while suspended upside-down. You don't have to perform in front of an audience in the way that Harry did, but when it comes to making excuses you can wriggle your way out of almost anything. For you, rationalizing things is a bit like walking through an open door.

10–15 Style is as important as substance today, or, as Marshall McLuhan put it in the 1960s: "The medium is the message." In today's terms, you are at times a master of spin, an expert at self-justification and at making excuses. At other times, propaganda, false trails, and disinformation are not for you. Your capacity for self-deception is inconsistent.

5–9 Poker, anyone? It's your call and you have a pair of threes. To win, you need to convince your opponent that your hand is stronger than it is and to do this you will have to justify to yourself the risk you are about to take. The table is waiting. All eyes are on you. You fold. Convincing yourself of the improbable is not always your strongest suit.

0–4 Unless you want to buck the trend, steer clear of a career in politics or espionage. You are an amateur as far as making excuses is concerned. Rather than blame other people, you like to take responsibility for your actions. You have little capacity to deceive yourself or other people by rationalizing things.

Rationalization — making excuses

In the world of business, when a company rationalizes they restructure and cut costs in an effort to become leaner and fitter, and therefore more competitive. Not so in psychoanalysis, where to rationalize means to find a reason or an excuse that justifies your feelings or something you've done and so conceals your unconscious motives. If you call in sick when you are not ill and tell yourself that other people always take time off, this is a "rationalization."

How we use rationalization

Rationalizations are commonly combined with other defenses. For example, a man who remarks that women are not as competitive as men (an example of projection) may bolster it with the rationalization that they'd prefer to be at home anyway. "I wouldn't want such an expensive car" (denial) may be followed with the thought that they're vulgar anyway (rationalization). We can rationalize someone else's behavior too: a woman who excuses her husband's drunken violence on the grounds that he is about to be made unemployed is rationalizing his behavior.

The "true" reason behind a neurotic symptom can be rationalized too—at least so say psychoanalysts. Thus, a person who is over cautious in the preparation of food to the point of obsession—scalding dishes, rewashing plates, bleaching cutlery—may be concealing a desire to poison those for whom they cook. The reaction-formation of excessive hygiene may then be bolstered with the rationalization that it's better to be safe than sorry.

To use a rationalization does not mean that you are being rational. On the contrary, a rationalization involves irrationally using a plausible cover story. A rationalization is not a form of logic—it is, rather, a piece of psycho-logic.

The next questionnaire measures the extent to which you intellectualize your feelings—another way of protecting yourself against what you feel.

Are you in touch with your feelings?

Do you know what you really feel or are you obsessed with being in control? Are you afraid of your emotions or can you share them with other people?

		Yes	No
1.	Does it embarrass you when other people are very emotional?	☐	☐
2.	If you were to cry during a sentimental movie, would you try to conceal your tears?	☐	☐
3.	Do you find it easy to see good and bad in the same person?	☐	☐
4.	If you lost a job, would you be open about it?	☐	☐
5.	Would you like to have a mind that worked as efficiently as a computer?	☐	☐
6.	Are you good at letting people know how you feel?	☐	☐
7.	Do you use the Internet for socializing more than for finding out things?	☐	☐
8.	When you have your hair cut, do you like to chat rather than to sit in silence?	☐	☐
9.	Given the choice, would you spend a week by yourself rather than with other people?	☐	☐
10.	Do you nearly always keep your feelings under tight control?	☐	☐
11.	Are you an easy person to get to know?	☐	☐
12.	As far as you're concerned, is intimacy something to be avoided?	☐	☐
13.	Do you sometimes laugh out loud when reading a book?	☐	☐
14.	Do you sometimes feel like a stranger in your own mind?	☐	☐
15.	Do you feel awkward kissing, hugging, or embracing in public?	☐	☐

16. X is a team player. Could this be you? ☐ ☐
17. Do you feel safest when you're on your own? ☐ ☐
18. Do you think that it's all right to manipulate other people for your own ends? ☐ ☐
19. Do you sometimes wonder where your thoughts come from? ☐ ☐
20. What you see is what you get. Is this true of you? ☐ ☐

Interpret your score

Give yourself one point for each answer that matches the key:

1. Yes	5. Yes	9. Yes	13. No	17. Yes
2. Yes	6. No	10. Yes	14. Yes	18. Yes
3. No	7. No	11. No	15. Yes	19. Yes
4. No	8. No	12. Yes	16. No	20. No

0–4 Your thoughts and feelings work hand in glove with each other. Whether it's anger, frustration, happiness, or sadness, when you feel something, you can usually show it—it rarely occurs to you to do otherwise. It's not that you wear your heart on your sleeve in a negative way, it's just that most of the time you know what you're feeling.

5–10 Joined-up thinking means that different parts of an organization know what the other parts are doing so that, in theory, everyone knows what's happening. Although you sometimes turn in on yourself, your thoughts are usually joined up with your feelings, so you don't often feel alienated from yourself or from other people. As a result, you usually express what you feel but can apply the brakes when you need to.

11–16 Some psychologists say that our personality is constructed not by something within us but by the situations we find ourselves in. In your case, for example, when you're under pressure you have a tendency to disown your feelings and to confuse this with having control over events. When you're not under pressure, on the other hand, you usually manage to stay in touch with your feelings.

17–20 In the same way that a person who is in quarantine is isolated from other people to prevent the spread of disease, so you tend to live in one world and your feelings tend to spend much of their time in another world. The trouble with cutting yourself off from your feelings like this is that you may forget where you put them or even if they're yours.

Isolation—not feeling your emotions

In science isolating variables is a virtue, as by keeping things separate you can more easily work out what's causing what. In psychoanalysis "isolation" has a different meaning, which is to disconnect yourself from your feelings so that you no longer experience them. The result of separating different parts of yourself like this is that you don't show or feel emotions such as disappointment, sadness, anger, or frustration when it would be natural to do so. By isolating experiences in this way—unemotionally accepting failure, detaching yourself from your anger and so forth—you deprive such experiences of their power to affect your ego directly and, in the process, disown them. This happens when we intellectualize our feelings—talking theoretically about the break down of a relationship, for example, rather than experiencing what we really feel. We also use isolation when we put contradictory thoughts and feelings into separate mental compartments to avoid conflict: to continue as usual while being unfaithful to a partner involves this kind of compartmentalization or splitting.

Splitting things up: for and against

One of the disadvantages of isolation is that we don't get to see the connections between things, because we're so busy separating them. Another disadvantage is that splitting things up like this leads us to see things in extremes—as all good or all bad, for instance—rather than as a mixture of the two. Another problem with detaching your thoughts and feelings from each another is that doing so may make you feel unreal. In particular, you may have thoughts and feelings which, because you have not previously acknowledged them, you don't recognize as being your own when you do experience them. Freud's patient Ernst Lanzer, known as the "Rat Man"—so called because of his obsession with an Eastern torture involving rats—had these kinds of intrusive thoughts, which he then tried to neutralize or "undo" by means of various rituals and compulsions.

Although isolating things from one another can help us to make sense of the world and manage our emotions more easily, splitting up our experiences too much can distort how we see things and lead to feelings of being fragmented.

The defense mechanisms on which the last three questionnaires in the next section are based reveal why, according to Freud, people are prejudiced, how he would have interpreted the Stockholm syndrome (the phenomenon of hostages becoming friendly with their captors), and what he thought lies behind religious rituals.

9 Freudian defense mechanisms that falsify reality

A recurrent Freudian theme is that we are unconsciously motivated to see things in the way in which we want to see them. To achieve this end, we sometimes go to extreme lengths: relocating parts of ourselves into other people, taking parts of other people into us, and sometimes putting our faith in a little magic.

Is it ever your fault?

Do you take responsibility for what you do? Or do you have a habit of blaming other people?

		Yes	No
1.	Do you think other people generally think the same way you do?	☐	☐
2.	When you meet someone new, can you sum them up in an instant?	☐	☐
3.	Do you tend not to notice other people's shortcomings?	☐	☐
4.	If you're in a bad mood, do you have a tendency to take it out on other people?	☐	☐
5.	Are you receptive to new ideas?	☐	☐
6.	Do you think that we pay insufficient attention to minority groups?	☐	☐
7.	Do you sometimes blame other people for your mistakes?	☐	☐
8.	Do you think some people are just born losers?	☐	☐
9.	Are you interested in what other people think?	☐	☐
10.	Are most of your problems the result of other people?	☐	☐
11.	"Let he who is without sin cast the first stone." Has this ever stopped you from doing so?	☐	☐
12.	Do you try hard to understand the views of people you disagree with?	☐	☐
13.	Do you prefer not to criticize other people?	☐	☐
14.	If you're in a good mood, does it surprise you if other people aren't in a good mood too?	☐	☐
15.	Are you generally tolerant of different viewpoints?	☐	☐
16.	Do you put your hand up quickly when it's your fault?	☐	☐

17. Would you say that there's a right and a wrong way of doing practically everything? ☐ ☐
18. Are you easily hurt by criticism? ☐ ☐
19. Too much discussion is bad for morale. Do you think so? ☐ ☐
20. Do you sometimes have an irrational feeling that you're being persecuted? ☐ ☐

Interpret your score

Give yourself one point for each answer that matches the key:

1. Yes	5. No	9. No	13. No	17. Yes
2. Yes	6. No	10. Yes	14. Yes	18. Yes
3. No	7. Yes	11. No	15. No	19. Yes
4. Yes	8. Yes	12. No	16. No	20. Yes

17–20 To attribute success to yourself and failure to other people is regarded by some psychologists as the healthy option (pass the driving test and it's because of you, fail and it's the examiner's fault). The trouble with the extreme version of this principle (blame first, ask questions later) is that it's easy to lose track of what belongs to you and what belongs to other people.

12–16 You are sometimes so averse to taking responsibility for your actions and so expert at attributing your shortcomings to other people that you don't even realize you're doing it. In contrast, although you feel better in the short term when you blame other people, when you take responsibility for what you do, you have a more accurate perception of reality.

6–11 Some people are prejudiced against people with beards, others find fault with those who are clean-shaven. In both cases, finding fault with someone else says as much about the person finding fault as it does about the other person. In your case, you're not immune from blaming other people—but what do you think about beards?

0–5 If you have a strong sense of who you are, this could be because you don't generally blame other people for your mistakes. Alternatively, having a strong sense of identity could be why you're not forever finding fault with other people. That's the trouble with correlations—you don't always know what's causing what. What is clear is that you usually take responsibility for what you do.

Projection—relocating your feelings

In the same way that anti-aging creams may reduce the appearance of wrinkles, so antidiscrimination laws are to some extent only cosmetic. Freudians see prejudice as a form of "projection," meaning that we unconsciously transfer or relocate a part of ourselves onto someone else. Although we sometimes project good things onto other people—idealizing someone, for example—much of projection is to do with attributing to other people what we don't like about ourselves (blaming other people for our own shortcomings, for example).

Everyday projection

We use projection in another way when we assume that someone else is thinking what we would be thinking if we were in their position. Often these projections turn out to be what we think the other person ought to be thinking. Parents do this when they project their values about religion, politics, and morality onto their children. Those who campaign to save the whale might be said to be projecting their infant experiences of being vulnerable and misunderstood onto the whales and then identifying with them.

When you use projection as a defense mechanism, you relocate your fears about yourself onto someone else. You might, for example, be worried about becoming overweight or unsure about your ability to be a good parent, or unconsciously concerned about losing your job. The answer to these fears, using projection, is to condemn those who are overweight, deprecate families experiencing problems, and blame the unemployed for not working. By projecting your fears onto other people you relieve yourself of your doubts about your own shortcomings.

Projective identification

Freud extended his work on projection into a theory of paranoia. Sometimes, he argued, we project our hatred onto other people and then come to believe that they hate us. This happens because we are identifying with what we have projected onto the other person. This was how Freud interpreted the delusions of persecution and injury at the hands of his physician that his contemporary Judge Daniel Paul Schreber described in his memoirs.

The next questionnaire is about taking parts of other people into you when you don't want to lose them or because you're frightened of them — what psychoanalysts call "introjection."

Are you a clone?

Is there only one of you in the world or do you share an identity with other people? To what extent do your thoughts belong to you?

		Yes	No
1.	When you were a child, did you ever have heroes or heroines?	☐	☐
2.	In an election, would you ever vote for a minor party?	☐	☐
3.	Are you always aware of what other people are feeling?	☐	☐
4.	Do you mind being the odd one out?	☐	☐
5.	Does the newspaper you read the most influence you politically?	☐	☐
6.	Are you easily able to resist the influence of other people's superstitions?	☐	☐
7.	Do you sometimes identify with a character in a movie?	☐	☐
8.	Does it concern you if you're the only person who holds a particular point of view?	☐	☐
9.	Are you ever a bit eccentric?	☐	☐
10.	Is there a particular group of people you like to identify with?	☐	☐
11.	Do you take movie critics seriously?	☐	☐
12.	Do you find that you change your mind depending on who you were last talking to?	☐	☐
13.	Have you given up many of the cultural values that you were brought up with?	☐	☐
14.	Do you belong to any clubs or societies?	☐	☐
15.	Do you influence most of your friends more than they influence you?	☐	☐

16. Are you, or have you ever been, a member of a cult? ☐ ☐
17. Have you ever modeled yourself on somebody else? ☐ ☐
18. Are you an independent type of person? ☐ ☐
19. Are you acutely sensitive to other people's moods? ☐ ☐
20. Do you hold very different moral values from those of your friends? ☐ ☐

Interpret your score

Give yourself one point for each answer that matches the key:

1. Yes	5. Yes	9. No	13. No	17. Yes
2. No	6. No	10. Yes	14. Yes	18. No
3. Yes	7. Yes	11. Yes	15. No	19. Yes
4. Yes	8. Yes	12. Yes	16. Yes	20. No

17–20 You are, like Dolly the sheep, who was cloned in a laboratory, a complete and utter clone at times—a composite of different people that you've known. The difference is that Dolly didn't need to worry about her identity, while you, with so many identities to choose from, sometimes feel as if you've got multiple personalities. Hardly surprising if, at times, you find it difficult to remain independent.

11–16 When you're not being independent, you're more of a chameleon than a clone, only instead of camouflaging yourself by changing the color of your skin you camouflage yourself by adopting other people's views. Enough of the natural history lesson though—it only applies to you some of the time anyway. Still, as you haven't got a long sticky tongue to catch insects, why be a reptile at all?

6–10 Question: how to reconcile the fact that you're not a clone (you like to think for yourself and you object to being told what you can and can't do) with the fact that you quite enjoy being in the majority? Easy. Minorities become larger exponentially (the so-called snowball effect), so you could end up always being in the majority.

0–5 There is nothing remotely clone-like about you—you've never been near a test tube in your life. In the same way that your DNA is a one-off combination of molecules passed down to you by your biological mother and father, so you have a unique personality and, for the most part, a strong sense of who you are. There is no one like you anywhere in the world.

Introjection—a way of holding onto things

Named after a bank robbery that took place in Sweden in 1973, the Stockholm syndrome describes the way that kidnap victims sometimes become friendly with their captors and adopt their values. In Freudian terms, this phenomenon is an example of "introjection," which means taking something into yourself, as opposed to relocating something outside yourself, as happens in projection. Patty Hearst in the 1960s in California and Natascha Kampusch, who was held for more than eight years in Austria, both made friends with their abductors, which may have helped them to keep safe.

How introjection works

The process of introjecting things into our minds is a natural part of our development—the psychological equivalent of ingesting food, just as projection is often the psychological equivalent of defecating. As babies, we absorbed our parents' moods and feelings toward us and then, when growing up, we cloned many of our ideas from their ideas—in particular, our conscience or superego. Over a period of time, we became independent of our parents because we had an introjected version of them in our mind.

Introjection works as a defense mechanism when, in order to contain anxiety, you take on the identity of someone you fear. Through a process of reversal you reduce the fear of something happening to you by doing it to someone else, either in reality or in fantasy. (Anna Freud described this as "identification with the aggressor.") This can sometimes be an attempt to control the past as when, in some cases, a person who has been sexually abused becomes an abuser or a victim of bullying copies those who have bullied them.

Introjection is an essential defense mechanism because in everyday life it prevents us from losing the things we value. It works hand in hand with projection, however, and together these two mechanisms distort each other. What you take in or introject of a person is inevitably colored by what you have previously projected onto that person: we see the world, in other words, through a swirling mist of our own projections and introjections—not at all in the accurate way in which we would like to think we do.

The next questionnaire is about belief in the power of mind over matter and measures whether you believe in magic or in reason.

How superstitious are you?

Are you ruled by reason or by ritual? Do you believe in science or do you believe in magic?

	Yes	No
1. Have you ever been allocated seat number 13 and considered trying to change it?	☐	☐
2. Do you think that apparently inexplicable happenings such as poltergeists can be explained in purely scientific terms?	☐	☐
3. Do you believe in karma?	☐	☐
4. Have you ever said "knock on wood" or "touch wood" and, not finding any, gone in search of it until you did?	☐	☐
5. Do you think that seeing ghosts is a figment of the imagination?	☐	☐
6. Do you believe in a spirit world?	☐	☐
7. Do you believe in telekinesis (the psychic power to influence inanimate objects with your mind)?	☐	☐
8. When you go to bed, do you always follow a set routine?	☐	☐
9. What about in the morning? Do you follow a set routine when you get up?	☐	☐
10. Do you have a lucky number?	☐	☐
11. Do you possess any lucky charms?	☐	☐
12. Some people regard astrology as a form of superstition. Do you think they're right?	☐	☐
13. Tarot card readers and other fortune-tellers have no special powers to see into the future. Do you agree with this sentiment?	☐	☐
14. Do certain numbers or colors have a special significance for you?	☐	☐

15. What about black cats? Do they have special   ☐ ☐
    significance?
16. People who claim to be able to get in touch with   ☐ ☐
    the dead are taking advantage of very vulnerable
    people for their own ends. Do you think so?
17. Do you believe in the power of prayer?   ☐ ☐
18. Does confessing things make you feel better?   ☐ ☐
19. Do you ever ask God to forgive you your sins?   ☐ ☐
20. Do you think that, as Karl Marx said, "religion is   ☐ ☐
    the opium of the people"?

Interpret your score

Give yourself one point for each answer that matches the key:

1. Yes	5. No	9. Yes	13. No	17. Yes
2. No	6. Yes	10. Yes	14. Yes	18. Yes
3. Yes	7. Yes	11. Yes	15. Yes	19. Yes
4. Yes	8. Yes	12. No	16. No	20. No

0–4 In the same way that Freud regarded himself as a scientist and was a fan of the Age of Reason (this didn't stop him from being convinced that he was going to die between the ages of 61 and 62), so you're the kind of person who likes to walk under ladders and to sit in seat number 13 just to prove that you're not superstitious. All good. But why so extreme?

5–10 You pride yourself on being logical, believing that potentially everything can be explained scientifically. (Look at the way people used to believe that the Devil curdled milk.) Sometimes, though, a dark cloud of superstition passes across your luminous scientific orb and your world is temporarily no longer bathed in the light of reason.

11–16 To see how superstitious you are occasionally capable of being, consider how some of your habits (This is how I've always done it) border on being rituals and how some of your routines (It works, so I'm going to keep doing it) have become superstitions. Give yourself a score and ask who's in charge. Surprising, eh?

17–20 Some sailors in the Middle Ages believed it to be unlucky to have a woman on board their ship. Something about making the sea angry or jealous. Yeah . . . right. Mermaids aside, instead of being on a journey of discovery and adventure, your life is becoming a voyage of superstition and ritual. To retain buoyancy, throw some of it overboard.

The magical defense of undoing

Dog owner to pooch: "Would you like a ginger snap or would you like a chocolate chip cookie?" Pooch's response: "Woof woof." Arguably there's not much difference between this and a child who sees a soft toy as being alive: the dog doesn't know what its owner is talking about and the soft toy isn't living. But in both cases their owners want the situation to be different, and the defense mechanism of "undoing" may help to explain why this is, as well as why in an age of exquisite feats of engineering, gene therapy, and nanotechnology there is still such a belief in the irrational, religion, and the paranormal.

"Undoing" is when you superstitiously perform a magic ritual in your mind to "cancel out" something you've already done or thought or to guard against something you think might happen. Freud described the illusion of making things "unhappen" like this as "negative magic." Psychoanalysts believe that our first experience of feeling so powerful was when as infants we were unable to distinguish ourselves from the external world and so omnipotently believed that we were causing things to happen.

We use ritual and superstition throughout our lives. Children use them when they say things like "fingers crossed" or when they refuse to tread on the cracks in the sidewalk. Adults use them, too, wearing a particular piece of clothing for good luck, not walking under ladders, throwing spilt salt over their left shoulder.

Observing rituals

Athletes are a group of people who appear to be very superstitious. When they prepare to compete, they go through elaborate rituals, sprinters settling into the blocks in their own idiosyncratic ways, tennis stars seemingly compelled to bounce the ball a prescribed number of times before they serve. Although, at one level, these routines are simply part of a practiced way of doing something, they are rituals to the extent that the person believes they cannot compete if they don't perform them.

Religion has always relied heavily upon ritual and superstition: sacrifice and the worship of fetish objects has a long tradition in many cultures and, even today, dressing up in fantastic clothes, group worship, the burning of incense, prayer, confession, abstinence, and fasting play central roles in many religions. Freud, who was both a Jew and an atheist, once described religion as "the universal obsessional neurosis of humanity." By this he meant that just as a person who is tied up with obsessions and compulsions feels that they have to perform certain rituals to avoid something catastrophic from happening, so religion (often with the promise of avoiding damnation) insists on the observance of rituals. In both cases, not carrying out the rituals induces feelings of guilt.

The writer and academic Mark Edmundson has summarized another of Freud's insights into religion (in addition to that of belief in religion being a wish-fulfilment to avoid death), in particular the lure of fundamentalism. In *Future of an Illusion* (1927) Freud argues that people look to autocratic religious and political leaders (Hitler, in Freud's experience) in an attempt to re-create the safety that they felt, or the safety that they would have liked to have felt, with their father. An all-loving superior being who sets rules that cannot be questioned infantilizes believers and makes them feel secure. As long as people lack insight into this psychological need to feel protected, fundamentalism will flourish.

Who's in control?

Undoing is, typically, an obsessional defense — compulsively counting up to certain numbers and doing things only in particular ways are common. Washing is a frequent compulsive ritual, too: both Pontius Pilate and Lady Macbeth tried to undo what they had done in this way. Undoing is a defense that most people make use of from time to time, but the irony of using magic and rituals to control our feelings — of believing, in effect, that we can exert mind over matter — is that we frequently end up being controlled by the spells that we're casting to try to control events.

Defense mechanisms: for and against

With the exception of sublimation, defense mechanisms are generally regarded rather negatively, though sometimes they work in our favor: denial can help us to focus on a task, isolation to think more clearly and objectively. Freud thought that one of the reasons that great art, music, and literature have the power to move us is that they allow us to experience the unconscious feelings that lie behind our everyday defenses. But he never said that any of us can live without using defense mechanisms; that's why it's a mistake, however well intentioned, to try to dismantle a person's defenses against their wishes.

BEFORE you get off the couch . . .

Now that you've completed the questionnaires in this book, I hope you have a good idea of how Freud would have interpreted some of the things you do, and some insight into why other people do some of the things they do, as well as being better placed to draw your own conclusions about Freud's ideas.

Terminating an analysis
In Freudian terms, terminating an analysis is like being weaned from the breast—though it's also a bit like leaving home. Like a parent, the analyst hopes that their analytic "child" has developed sufficient inner resources to sustain them through their life. Like a child, the patient leaves behind the person who has helped them to develop their ego. In order to work through any feelings that may otherwise surface after the analysis has ceased—for example, the feeling of being abandoned—termination is prepared for over a period of months, the number of sessions being gradually reduced to one or two per week.

Analysis terminable and interminable
Is termination necessary? The not entirely logical answer is that it's usually thought that a person should stand on their own two feet. But there are many other relationships in life where people are, at least, interdependent—most long-term relationships, for example—and we're not against people being on insulin for life. In his essay "Analysis Terminable and Interminable" (1937) Freud discusses the difficulty of saying that an analysis is ever complete and recommends that analysts should themselves be re-analyzed every five years. The psychotherapist Anthony Storr thought that rather than being "cured" people become better able to deal with their problems.

Developments in psychoanalysis

During the twentieth century, many people took up Freud's ideas and modified them. Freud's contemporary Carl Jung (1875–1961) argued that Freud had overemphasized the role of sex and believed instead that human beings have a drive toward experiencing the spiritual side of life—what he called the "religious function." Another contemporary, Alfred Adler (1870–1937), thought that we're motivated by the need for power: because we're so powerless as children, we spend the rest of our life striving to achieve control—the "will to power." Early in the century, the Hungarian psychoanalyst Melanie Klein (1882–1960) started working with children, speculating from her analysis of their play that their intense, at times irrational, feelings of love and hate get carried forward into adult life. In contrast, Freud's daughter, Anna Freud (1895–1982), who also worked with children, focused on the ego and its mechanisms of defense, while "object relations theorists" such as Donald Winnicott (1896–1971) argued that we have a drive to be with and to relate to other people or "objects." Likewise, in the Unites States pioneering neo-Freudians such as Karen Horney (1885–1952), Erich Fromm (1900–1980), and Harry Stack Sullivan (1892–1949) focused on the influence of culture on the individual. In France, the maverick psychoanalyst Jacques Lacan (1901–1981) upset the psychoanalytic establishment by arguing that the unconscious exists not in our head but outside of us in our language and culture. This was of interest to feminist psychoanalysts, as it helped to explain, without reference to anatomy, the unconscious mechanisms by which power is transmitted from one generation to the next.

The Freud Wars

According to the historian Phyllis Grosskurth, in order to try to preserve psychoanalysis in its original form and protect it against its critics, in 1912 Freud formed an inner circle of loyal thinkers composed of himself and six others (the "Secret Committee"), to each of whom he gave a ring. Although he became a celebrity, lecturing in 1909 at Clark University, Massachusetts, Freud continued to draw criticism from within psychoanalysis from women such as Karen Horney, who accused him of not understanding them. In the 1950s and '60s, the psychologist Hans Eysenck and the philosopher Karl Popper challenged the scientific credibility of psychoanalysis, and the immunologist Peter Medawar claimed in 1975 that "psychoanalytic theory is the most stupendous intellectual confidence trick of the twentieth century." In the same year, Paul Roazen revealed, for the first time publicly, that Freud (in violation of his own code of conduct) had analyzed his daughter Anna, and exposed, too, how the Freud legend had been manipulated by the psychoanalytic establishment. In 1984 Jeffrey Masson, erstwhile curator of the Freud archives, published his bestseller *The Assault on Truth*, in which he charged that Freud had dropped the seduction theory because of hostile criticism from his medical colleagues. Gloria Steinem's feminist parody "What If *Freud* Were *Phyllis*? or, The Watergate of the Western World," published in the 1990s, explored what Freudian theory would have looked like if it had been written by a woman, complete with "testyria," womb envy, and under-confident young men facing overwhelming female superiority in a fictional matriarchy. There have been many others who have taken up arms against Freud in what have become known as the Freud Wars. Freud's arch-critic Todd Dufresne includes among them: Mikkel Borch-Jacobson, Frank Cioffi, Frederick Crews, Edward Shorter, Frank Sulloway, Peter Swales, Sebastiano Timpanaro, and Richard Webster. Their criticisms are mostly based on historical, textual, and scientific analyses of what Freud wrote, though, in some cases, these are entwined with attempts to discredit his character. Hostilities have, if anything, intensified in the twenty-first century: there's no sign of a truce just yet.

The Freudian paradox

If each world leader had their own psychoanalyst, they might be less inclined to act out their unconscious childhood fantasies on a global scale. Although this particular daydream may not be a reality, in view of the intellectual and emotional opposition that Freud generated, it's hard to understand why his ideas took root so firmly in the public consciousness. One student told me he thought it was because Freud wrote about sex and death in the way the press often does. Psychoanalysis also offered an alternative view of the world at a time when religious belief was declining. Equally hard to explain is why Freud, who was trained in the scientific method—and so believed that everything has a cause that can be traced—developed a theory that was so unscientific. Nowhere was he less scientific than in his formulation of a theory of child development, as he never worked with children. (In the case of Herbert Graf, known as "Little Hans," the three year-old boy who developed a fear of horses, Freud met him only once as a child, his father acting as an intermediary.) Nevertheless, most subsequent work on motherhood and childcare (for example, John Bowlby's influential theory of attachment) has its origin in Freud's belief that early childhood experiences unconsciously influence adult behavior. It's ironic, too, that Freud should have been vilified for not understanding women and yet psychotherapies that owe their existence to his development of a talking cure are so well represented by women. In both cases it can be argued that these represent attempts to correct Freud's mistakes but, even if that's true, the concepts being used to do so are ones formulated by Freud.

Whether Freud will be remembered in the same way as Copernicus and Darwin, with whom he compared himself, remains to be seen. It has been said that each in their own way challenged a childlike view of the world: Copernicus by showing us that the sun doesn't revolve around us, but we around it; Darwin by revealing that there is no discontinuity between us and other species; and Freud by exploring the unconscious mind that motivates us to see the world in the way we want to see it.

Final analysis

In theory, no one is ever fully analyzed. Since we can always learn more about ourselves, an analysis is always incomplete. Although Freud set a time limit on his treatment and terminated his first and second periods of analysis, his patient Sergei Pankejeff, known as the "Wolf Man"—so called because of a dream he reported—went on seeing a therapist until he was well into his eighties. Making what is unconscious conscious is an ongoing process.

Bibliography and further reading

Freud and Freudian theory

Bateman, Anthony and Holmes, Jeremy. *Introduction to Psychoanalysis: Contemporary Theory and Practice*. London: Routledge, 1995.

Brown, J.A.C. *Freud and the Post-Freudians*. Harmondsworth: Penguin Books, 1964.

Edmundson, Mark. *The Death of Sigmund Freud: Fascism, Psychoanalysis and the Rise of Fundamentalism*. London: Bloomsbury, 2007.

Freud, Anna. *The Ego and the Mechanisms of Defence*. London: Hogarth Press, 1936.

Freud, Sigmund. *The Standard Edition of the Complete Psychological Works of Sigmund Freud*, Vols. i–xxiv. London: Vintage, 2001.

Frosh, Stephen. *The Politics of Psychoanalysis: An Introduction to Freudian and Post-Freudian Theory*. London: MacMillan Education, 1987.

Gay, Peter. *Freud: A Life for Our Time*. New York: W.W. Norton, 1988.

Grosskurth, Phyllis. *The Secret Ring: Freud's Inner Circle and the Politics of Psychoanalysis*. New York: Addison Wesley, 1991.

Kline, Paul. *Psychology and Freudian Theory: An Introduction*. London: Methuen, 1984.

Stafford-Clark, David. *What Freud Really Said*. Harmondsworth: Penguin Books, 1965.

Storr, Anthony. *Freud*. Oxford: Oxford University Press, 1989.

Wollheim, Richard. *Freud* (Second Edition). London: Fontana Press, 1991.

Psychoanalysis

Casement, Patrick. *On Learning from the Patient*. London: Tavistock Publications, 1985.

— *Further Learning from the Patient*. Abingdon: Taylor and Francis, 1990.

Chodorow, Nancy. *The Reproduction of Mothering: Psychoanalysis and the Sociology of Gender*. Berkeley: University of California Press, 1978.

Elliott, Anthony. *Psychoanalytic Theory: An Introduction*. Oxford: Blackwell, 1994.

Heimann, P. "On Countertransference." *International Journal Of Psychoanalysis* 31: 81-84, 1950.

Irigaray, L. *The Sex Which is Not One*, Ithica, NY: Cornell University Press, 1985.

Malcolm, Janet. *Psychoanalysis: The Impossible Profession*. London: Pan Books, 1982.

— *In the Freud Archives*. London: Fontana, 1986.

Mitchell, Juliet. *Psychoanalysis and Feminism*. Harmondsworth: Penguin Books, 1974.

Rycroft, Charles. *A Critical Dictionary of Psychoanalysis* (Second Edition). London: Penguin Reference, 1995.

Winnicott, Donald W. *The Piggle: An Account of the Psychoanalytic Treatment of a Little Girl*. Harmondsworth: Penguin Books, 1980.

Freudian criticism

Dufresne, Todd. *Killing Freud*. London: Continuum, 2003.

— *Against Freud: Critics Talk Back*. Stanford: Stanford University Press, 2007.

Eysenck, Hans J. *Decline and Fall of the Freudian Empire*. Harmondsworth: Penguin Books, 1985.

Forrester, John. *Dispatches from the Freud Wars: Psychoanalysis and Its Passions*. Cambridge MA: Harvard University Press, 1997.

Masson, Jeffrey M. *The Assault on Truth: Freud's Suppression of the Seduction Theory*. New York: Farrar, Straus and Giroux, 1984.

— *Against Therapy*. London: Fontana, 1990.

— *Final Analysis*. London: Harper Collins, 1991.

Roazen, Paul. *Freud and His Followers*. London: Allen Lane, 1976.

Steinem, Gloria. "What if *Freud* Were *Phyllis*? or, The Watergate of the Western World," in *Moving Beyond Words*. London: Bloomsbury, 1994.

Webster, Richard. *Why Freud Was Wrong: Sin, Science, and Psychoanalysis*. New York: Basic Books, 1995.

**PSYCHE
BOOKS**

The study of the mind: interactions, behaviors, functions. Developing and learning our understanding of self. Psyche Books cover all aspects of psychology and matters relating to the head.